GW01086730

Death of a Rose

Who Killed Hilda Murrell?

Hilda Murrell

Death of a Rose-Grower

Who Killed Hilda Murrell?

by Graham Smith

CECIL WOOLF · LONDON

First published 1985
© 1985 Graham Smith

Cecil Woolf Publishers, 1 Mornington Place, London NW1 7RP
Tel: 01-387 2394

ISBN 0-900821-75-2 paperback edition
ISBN 0-900821-76-0 hardback edition

Sequence of Events

January 1983	Private detectives begin snooping on Sizewell B objectors.
March 1984	Downing Street panics over *Belgrano* leaks.
Wed., 21 March, c. 12.30 pm	Hilda Murrell returns home unexpectedly. She confronts an intruder in her home and is abducted in her own car.
12.45-1.10 pm	Miss Murrell's car is seen being driven erratically towards Hunkington Moat area.
Later that afternoon	Two boys steal the tax disc from Miss Murrell's car, which has apparently crashed into a ditch.
5.20 pm	Local farmer notifies off-duty police officer about the car in the ditch. Police visit the scene within an hour. They search the immediate area but find nothing wrong.
Thur., 22 March, 3.30 pm	Another local farmer, Ian Scott, walks through the copse where Miss Murrell's body was later found. He does not see anything amiss and is convinced the body was not there.
Later Thursday evening	Local people see lights moving in the copse.
Fri., 23 March, 7 pm	Police visit Miss Murrell's home after the abandoned car is again reported to them, but notice nothing wrong.
Sat., 24 March, early morning	Increasingly concerned, police again visit Miss Murrell's home and search the building. Later that morning, neighbours enter and notice immediately the house has been burgled.
10.20 am	Police and gamekeeper's wife find Miss Murrell's body in the copse. She has been stabbed repeatedly. Police then visit Miss Murrell's house for the third time.

Contents

Illustrations

Preface

Most 'instant' books are instantly forgettable. I hope interest in *Death of a Rose-Grower* will last for at least as long as the murderer of Hilda Murrell remains at large.

This is a book which raises more questions than it answers. There are many lines of inquiry I would like to have pursued given more time and greater resources.

I hope the facts presented here will encourage readers to ask their own questions—and carry on asking them until Hilda Murrell's brutal killer is brought to justice.

St Mabyn, Cornwall   Graham Smith
22 March 1985

Acknowledgements

I would like to thank Cecil and Jean Woolf for encouraging me to write this book. Greg Neale read and improved the manuscript. Alan Peach of the West Mercia Constabulary fielded my questions with patience and good humour.

G. S.

Hilda's Tale

THE STORY OF A ROSE-GROWER

Hilda Murrell was born at Eaton Cottage in the Column area of Shrewsbury on 3 February 1906. Her parents, Owen and Lily, with her grandfather, Edwin Murrell, ran the family firm of Murrell's Nurseries from which Hilda derived her life-long passion for the natural world of flowers and conservation.

Owen and Lily were by no means wealthy, but Hilda was a bright, studious child and won a scholarship to Shrewsbury High School where she was head girl. She went on to read English, Mediaeval Languages and French at Newnham College, Cambridge. She graduated from there in 1928 and joined the family firm. She remained at Murrell's Nurseries for more than thirty years, her academic qualities adjusting swiftly to the needs of the commercial world. The business, like her flowers, flourished. Murrell's flowers were highly sought, even by the Royal gardeners at Buckingham Palace. Hilda Murrell specialised in old rose species and miniature roses and travelled Europe, building up a vast network of friends. She won scores of prizes at local and national flower shows. Her name will be remembered in the rose called Hilda Murrell. Mr David Austin, a leading rose grower, said: 'It is of the purest shining pink, and its flowers are very nearly perfect.' During the war Miss Murrell helped raise money for Jewish refugees from Czechoslovakia and found them homes in Shropshire and the Welsh Marches.

After the war Owen Murrell died. Hilda and her cousin, Leslie Murrell, took over the responsibility of running the nursery. Leslie Murrell's daughter, Carolyn Davies, is the only surviving relative of Hilda Murrell who still lives in the Shrewsbury area.

In 1962 Hilda and Leslie sold the original Column nursery site for housing development. Hilda opened a new business, Portland Nurseries, at a site on the A5 by-pass. At the same time she helped launch the Shropshire Conservation Trust. In 1970 she sold the nursery to Brian Murphy, who ran it with the TV gardener and author, Percy Thrower. She then retired.

Hilda Murrell was 65 but had no intention of giving up

her community activities. She was conservative and sensible in her dress; rather shy and retiring but could also be quite forceful when necessary. Some of her friends thought Hilda Murrell was a bit eccentric. Most thought her a typical, shining example of traditional Britishness.

The Conservation Trust took up much of her time. She had been a member of its governing council for eight years and began a campaign of fund-raising Christmas card sales which today has grown into a large-scale annual operation. Miss Murrell became concerned about the threat of nuclear war. She supported the European Nuclear Disarmament group, the Shrewsbury Peace Group and the Nuclear Weapons Freeze Advertising Campaign. She was also actively supporting the Monument Trust, a national body which raises money for tree-planting, the Llanymynech Rocks Nature Reserve, on whose management committee she served, and the Shropshire branch of the Council for the Protection of Rural England, whose amenities sub-committee she chaired. She was, in addition, a supporter of the Campaign for Nuclear Disarmament and Greenpeace. In October 1983 she travelled from Shrewsbury to London to take part in a huge demonstration organised by CND against cruise missiles.

Much of her leisure time was spent at what she called her 'shack', a wooden chalet at Llanymynech, near Oswestry, where she walked, watched birds and tended her garden. It was at this weekend retreat that Hilda Murrell developed her views on nuclear power, which she was convinced was an unnecessary evil. She was particularly concerned about the government's plans for a pressurised-water reactor at Sizewell in Suffolk and hoped to present a paper in evidence at the Sizewell B public inquiry. In recent years, with some help, she had learned about nuclear physics. Hilda was particularly concerned about the problems posed by the disposal of radioactive waste. She wrote regularly to government ministers, even to the Prime Minister, outlining her objections to government policy. She also wrote frequently to her two favourite newspapers, *The Times* and *The Guardian*, putting the case for conserving the natural environment and attacking plans for nuclear power.[1]

By 21 March Hilda Murrell's paper on Sizewell had been typed. She nevertheless continued working on it and wrote in her diary: 'Started polishing and correcting paper. Eliminated 16 lines from first six pages. Not enough though.'[2]

Over the weekend of 17-18 March 1984 Hilda Murrell was telephoned by a friend to make an appointment for Wednesday, 21 March; they were to meet for lunch, to discuss gardening.

On the morning of Wednesday, the 21st, Hilda Murrell left her detached home at Ravenscroft, 52 Sutton Road, Shrewsbury. She drove into the Abbey Foregate area of Shrewsbury in her white Renault 5, registration number LNT 917W, to withdraw £50 from the bank and buy some groceries at Safeways.[3]

Shortly after 12 noon she returned home and parked her car on the gravel driveway. But she did not go indoors straight away. Instead, she crossed the road and visited Mrs Frances O'Connor, whom she had known for most of her life, to settle a small debt for some charity draw tickets. Mrs O'Connor told me that Miss Murrell seemed happy and her usual contented self. 'She was a very reserved person, a bit old-fashioned perhaps—she always had been and I went to school with her—but on the day she came to see me there was never the slightest suggestion that anything was wrong,' said Mrs O'Connor. 'I've heard some people putting about the idea that she thought someone was after her. It's utter rubbish.'[4] That was the last time that Hilda Murrell was seen when it can be stated with absolute certainty that she was alive.

Almost everything that happened next has become the subject of fierce controversy, intense speculation and the stuff of a bizarre, intriguing political thriller.

A Detective's Tale

On 30 March 1984, Police Constable Cedric Harold
McCormick of the West Mercia Constabulary swore an oath
at Shrewsbury Magistrates' Court: 'At 6.15 pm on Satur-
day, 24 March 1984 I attended the mortuary of the Royal
Shrewsbury hospital,' he said, 'and there met Mr Graham
Hartley Davies, a Company Director of Pontesford House,
Pontesford, Shropshire. At the mortuary he was shown a
body of a female which he identified as being that of Hilda
Murrell.'[1]

The Coroner, Colonel David Crawford Clarke, opened
the inquest and adjourned the hearing to 25 July. In fact,
the inquest was not held until 5 December, when Detective
Chief Superintendent David Cole, the head of West Mercia's
Criminal Investigation Department, told the Coroner: 'I am
prepared to disclose as much evidence as possible to assist
the inquest.

'I am not, however, prepared to disclose all the evidence
in my possession. This is in no way an attempt to conceal
anything, but I must be in a position to put evidence to a
suspect which has not been previously released so that the
accuracy of anything a suspect tells me may be tested.'

This chapter is devoted to the information released by
police as their inquiry progressed. It is presented without
comment. Det. Chief Supt Cole says the first he knew of the
the murder was on Saturday, 24 March when he was
'informed of a suspicious death' near Shrewsbury. For Mr
Cole, it was the first of many 130-mile round-trips made
each day from the West Mercia police headquarters at
Worcester to Shrewsbury.

He told the inquest into Miss Murrell's death that he
went to a small coppice, known locally as The Moat, at
Hunkington, at 1.30 pm, where he found 'the body of an
elderly white female, approximately 500 yards across a
corn field, off a minor road that runs from Haughmond
Hill towards Withington'. She had been stabbed repeatedly.
Mr Cole continued: 'The body was lying next to a tree on
its right side, with the right arm bent and lying in front of
the body, and the left arm lying behind the body. The

10

right leg was also slightly bent and lying underneath the
left leg.'

Det. Chief Supt Cole said that Miss Murrell was wearing
a brown woollen coat, two jumpers and an underslip. One
stocking was found on the left foot and the other close to
the body.

'Also close to the body we found a skirt and a suspender
belt,' he said. 'She was not wearing knickers.'

Hilda Murrell's white Renault was in a roadside ditch
500 yards away.

'Dealing with the question of this vehicle,' continued Mr
Cole, 'my initial inquiries showed that the car had been
seen in the ditch in the position in which it was found on
the afternoon of 21 March 1984 by a local farmer who had
notified the police.

'Officers had attended the scene where the vehicle was
within an hour, but they found that there were no suspicious
circumstances.

'There was only superficial damage to the car and there
was no apparent danger or obstruction to any member of
the public.

'They made a preliminary search of the immediate area,
but there were no signs of injuries to anyone within the
vehicle and, at that stage, they decided to take no further
action.'

Det. Chief Supt Cole continued: 'On the afternoon of
23 March 1984, there had been a further call concerning
this vehicle as it was still in the position noted on the Wednesday. As a result, police officers that evening went to
Miss Murrell's home.

'They couldn't get any reply at the house and a search
was organised the following morning.

'The result of that was that the body of Miss Murrell
was found by police in company with a gamekeeper's wife
on the morning of Saturday, 24 March 1984. The body
was found at 10.25 am.'[2]

The gamekeeper's wife was Mrs Chris Randall. The body
was actually found by her dogs, a black labrador, Jet,
and terrier, Smudge. Mrs Randall's husband, Vic, managed
the 2,000-acre Sundorne Estate for its owner, John de
Quincey. Mrs Randall had volunteered to help police
because her husband was out. She and the policemen spent

about 20 minutes searching other woods before turning to
The Moat coppice.[3]

On discovery of Miss Murrell's body, police began a
detailed search of the surrounding area.

'This subsequent search led to the finding of the
deceased's moccasin type boots which were approximately
200 yards from the body in the corn field between the
road and the coppice,' said Det. Chief Supt Cole. 'They
were about 20 yards apart.'

He continued: 'Also in a different area, adjacent to the
hedge which led away from the Haughmond Hill-Withington
road, where the vehicle was found, towards the coppice
across the top of a corn field, further articles were found.
Her spectacles were found on the Haughmond Hill side of
that hedge. They were broken. Her wide-brimmed brown-
coloured hat and a knife was actually found in a ditch on
that side of the hedge. It is suspected, but not confirmed,
that the knife had been removed from the kitchen of Miss
Murrell's house.'[4]

The spot where Miss Murrell's body was found is an
area of unspoiled countryside, tucked away down a
network of narrow lanes. Many of the roads are bordered
by steeply falling banks, ditches and hedges. Police told

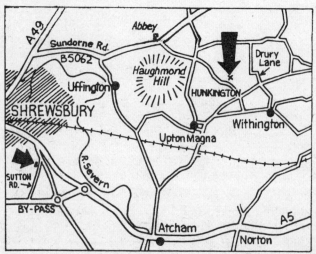

Arrowed on the left is Miss Murrell's home and on the right the spot
where her body was discovered.

reporters that it was not unusual for cars to slip into ditches and their early theories included the possibility that Miss Murrell had been attacked while on a nature walk. Only later did it become clear that she had been abducted.[5]

Det. Chief Supt Cole visited Miss Murrell's home and examined it carefully. 'I should also add that it was examined in great detail by forensic scientists and my own scientific officers,' he said.

'I found no evidence of forcible entry, but formed the opinion that access could have been gained to the house via an insecure door.

'I saw clear evidence that a struggle had taken place inside the house, and that a thorough and systematic search had been made of the premises.

'The front downstairs curtains were drawn and the electric light in one of the rooms had been left on. There were no signs of a sexual assault, but I did find signs within the house that there had been some sexual activity involving Miss Murrell, and this was later confirmed by forensic examination.'

Outside Miss Murrell's home police found a footprint. It was very clear and came from an imported, trainer-type shoe.

Det. Chief Supt Cole believes that, on returning home from her shopping, Miss Murrell either disturbed an intruder or was followed into the house by her killer. Police believe the motive for the crime was the theft of £50 cash. They told reporters that Miss Murrell's telephone wires had been ripped from the wall socket.[6]

'Once inside the house,' continued Mr Cole, 'Miss Murrell apparently had time to change from her outdoor clothing and put away some of her shopping. There is then evidence that a struggle with the offender ensued. This struggle took place upstairs.'[7]

Police believe Miss Murrell was tied to a bannister at the top of the stairs while the intruder searched her home. They think he even helped himself to a can of beer from her drinks cabinet.

Miss Murrell was then abducted and driven away in her own car. 'From inquiries I have directed,' continued Det. Chief Supt Cole, 'it is quite clear that Miss Murrell was driven away from her home by a man driving her car with

Miss Murrell in the passenger seat. This journey travelled through Sutton Road to the Column Island to Monkmoor traffic lights and along Monkmoor Road. Police believe the car was being driven in an erratic fashion.

'From there, along Telford Way to the Heathgates Island, along Sundorne Road and up to Haughmond Hill, turning right into Haughmond Hill to Hunkington Road.

'This journey almost certainly commenced shortly before 1 pm on Wednesday, 21 March and took approximately 20 minutes to complete.'

Det. Chief Supt Cole has several witnesses who remember seeing Miss Murrell's car as it made its way out of Shrewsbury. One of them, a motorcyclist, recalls pulling up behind the Renault when it stopped at temporary traffic lights.

'He is quite sure,' said Mr Cole, 'that he saw Miss Murrell as a passenger in this vehicle, driven by a male person at that particular time.

'The vehicle travelled towards Haughmond Hill and drew away from his vision. A retired farm labourer, who lives in Upton Magna, passed along the Hunkington Road at approximately 5 minutes to one on the day in question. 'He does not remember seeing the Renault as he walked towards Sandy Bank turn, that is away from The Moat, where the body was found.

'However, on his return journey about 15 minutes later, he does remember that the Renault was parked on the side of the road in the position in which it was subsequently found when the police officers were called to it.'

Det. Chief Supt Cole believes the journey from Miss Murrell's home took place between 12.45 pm and 1.10 pm. 'The Renault car came to rest approximately one and a quarter miles along Hunkington Lane, having collided with both sides of the banked verges of the roadway before coming to rest.

'There was only superficial damage to the vehicle and an unsuccessful attempt had obviously been made to drive the vehicle out of the ditch.'

Police think Miss Murrell then snatched the car keys and tried to make a run for it. Her attacker caught her and killed her.

Police later found a 'Hamlet' cigar wrapper in the Renault which they believe belonged to the murderer. Miss Murrell

was a non-smoker. Police also found a small tent-peg which
had been wired in such a way that it could have been a
poacher's snare.[8]

Mr Cole says the police investigation of Miss Murrell's
murder has been hampered by her personality. 'Clearly
this lady had the respect and affection of friends and
relations,' he said, 'but it seems her nature did not allow
these relationships to develop to such an extent that any
person knew the intimate details of the patterns of her
life.'[9]

He continued: 'Therefore, the police have experienced
considerable difficulty with regard to establishing her
exact possessions, clothing and her frequent and regular
movements.

'It was probably for this reason that she was not reported missing to the police, bearing in mind the added
difficulty that she had a second home in the Llanymynech
area, and she was known to frequently visit that area.

'In stating my conclusions about the likely sequence and
pattern of events surrounding Miss Murrell's death, it is
necessary to make assumptions and deductions.

'While it is accepted that these may not necessarily be
100 per cent accurate, they are nevertheless based on considerable experience and a thorough review of the facts.'

Some of the facts upon which Det. Chief Supt Cole
based his evidence at the inquest had come from a hypnotist. Two months after the murder he told reporters that
'more than one' witness had undergone hypnosis 'under
strictly controlled conditions to elucidate information
which they were unable to recall through the normal
memory processes. It is the first time in my experience I
have found it necessary to use hypnosis during an
investigation.' The hypnosis had been performed by 'a
medically qualified person' and had brought 'some measure
of success.'[10]

Criticism of police methods in the Yorkshire Ripper case a
a few years earlier had encouraged the West Mercia detectives
to record every snippet of information about Hilda Murrell's
murder on computer. Photo-fit pictures of an unknown
suspect were released at an early stage of the inquiry.[11]

Just five days after the killing, police thought someone
locally might be shielding the murderer. Det. Chief Supt

Cole told reporters of his fear that someone might be with-holding information. At the same time police issued this description of the wanted man: aged about 30, 5 ft 6 in to 5 ft 7 in tall, slim with fair hair. On 2 April 1984, less than a fortnight after the discovery of Miss Murrell's body, police issued this photo-fit picture:

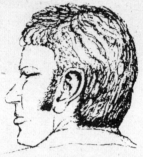

The picture was accompanied by this description. Police said the wanted man was 'white, aged between 25 and 40, well-built and with broadish shoulders. He has medium to dark brown collar-length hair, neatly groomed, with a slight fringe. He is clean shaven and has a narrow face and sallow complexion.' The killer was scruffily dressed in either a grey suit or blue-grey jacket and wore light coloured, but dirty, training shoes.

By this time more than 120 police officers were involved in the murder hunt, looking, they believed, for a man seen running along Sundorne Road and in the Heathgates Island area.

Two days after releasing the photo-fit pictures and description, detectives themselves donned grey suits and re-enacted the part of the 'running-man'. Hundreds of people were questioned about the man and Det. Chief Supt Cole told reporters: 'It is difficult to understand why he has not come forward if he is an innocent party.' Police said later they had further sightings of the 'running man' heading back along Telford Way and appealed to anyone who may have given him a lift. A week later, police were looking for an elderly couple seen in a light green Morris Traveller parked near the scene where Miss Murrell's body was found.[12]

In May, Det. Chief Supt Cole appealed for information about a man wearing a blue anorak. 'The garment's main feature is a metal D-ring in the centre of the back,' he said. 'A witness who saw the man driving Miss Murrell's car has described the anorak.'[13]

In July police issued a new photo-fit picture:

The wanted man was described as being 30-35, of medium to large build and broad shoulders. He had dark brown hair, which may have been showing traces of grey, with deep-set, dark eyes. He was wearing 'blue-top' clothing, presumably an anorak.[14]

By this time the police had gathered an enormous amount of information about Hilda Murrell's killing. They had also been in touch with Interpol (International Police Liaison Organisation). The Shrewsbury public were asked to forward information about a red Ford Escort car seen in the vicinity of Miss Murrell's home on the day of her abduction and later in the area where her body was found. Police did not know if it was in any way connected with the murder, but wanted the driver to come forward so that he could be eliminated from inquiries.

But perhaps one of the more intriguing moves was the police appeal to America's Federal Bureau of Investigation (FBI) in September 1984. This was reported in the *Shropshire Star* at the time[15] but not picked up by national newspapers until December.

West Mercia police asked the FBI's behavioural science research department to draw a 'personality picture' of the killer. The FBI report, said police, indicated that the murderer was a white male in his 30s.

'He is probably an unsocialised and withdrawn individual,'

B

said Det. Chief Supt Cole. 'He is probably an habitué of
local licensed premises and is likely to be an unskilled
worker. There is little doubt he made his way to Miss
Murrell's house on foot and it is therefore likely he does
not own a vehicle.

'It is also thought likely he may have some knowledge of
the attacked premises where his motive was primarily
burglary.'

Police inquiries in Sutton Road, where Miss Murrell lived,
found that 113 unidentified people had visited the area in
the days immediately preceding her murder. Police travelled
the country in their attempt to eliminate these people from
their inquiries.

One difficulty they encountered was that a group of door-
to-door salesmen from Nottingham visited Sutton Road
during the course of the week in which Miss Murrell died.
Detectives subsequently interviewed 370 salesmen.

Police also checked on the movements of 290 absentees
from local schools and colleges. By the time of the inquest,
only three people in Sutton Road on the day of the
murder remained untraced. At one stage police had nearly
3,600 potential suspects, for reasons, according to Det.
Chief Supt Cole, 'of their description, previous convictions
for like offences or evidence based upon their *modus
operandi.*

'These have all been researched by local and national
intelligence agencies. The antecedents of those nominated
have been analysed having regard to the age, appearance
of the suspect and varying elements of the *modus operandi*
disclosed in this murder investigation.

'This has resulted in a total of 962 persons being
processed in the major incident room at Shrewsbury.'

By the time of the inquest, about half of these suspects
had been interviewed; the rest were 'subject to an on-going
inquiry.'

Nine months after the murder, and having reviewed all
the available evidence, Det. Chief Supt Cole told the inquest
he was left with 'the inescapable conclusion that this was an
offence of burglary. The offender was after, in the main,
cash.'[16]

This remains the police position today. They are no
closer to catching Hilda Murrell's killer.

A Doctor's Tale

WHAT THE PATHOLOGIST FOUND

The Home Office pathologist who examined Miss Murrell's
body was Dr Peter Acland, from Edgbaston, Birmingham.
The coroner has consistently refused to release the full
report of the post-mortem examination; an examination
which led to the conclusion that Miss Murrell died of hypothermia (abnormally low body temperature) after having
been repeatedly stabbed.

Hypothermia is extremely difficult to detect. One expert[1]
told me that in the case of Miss Murrell, whose body is
presumed to have lain unnoticed for three days, it would
be almost impossible to prove medically that she died from
hypothermia.

Miss Murrell's relatives were not told they could have an
independent examination of the body and any speculation
that she might have been drugged must remain just that —
unsubstantiated speculation.

Dr Acland did not find any unnatural chemicals in Miss
Murrell's body. If he had, it might have been possible to
establish more precisely *when* she died.

But at the inquest Dr Acland could say only that he
expected Miss Murrell would have died from hypothermia
five to ten hours after she was stabbed. This would put the
time of death at somewhere between 6 pm and midnight
on Wednesday, 21 March.

On 10 January 1985 Dr Acland wrote to *The Times*,
defending his evidence at the inquest into Miss Murrell's
death, and denying anything unduly 'mysterious' about the
killing. 'I don't know who killed Miss Murrell,' he said,
'but I have a strong suspicion that some two-penny half-
penny thief is gloating over a pint of beer in a pub not many
miles from Shrewsbury about all this media interest.'

A month earlier, Dr Acland had been required to disclose
publicly as much information about Miss Murrell's death as
he could. This is what he told the inquest:[2]

> On Saturday, 24 March 1984 I was called at 11.30 am
> by Chief Supt Cole of the West Mercia police, and
> together with him inspected the body of Hilda Murrell

that was found in a copse near Hunkington.

She was wearing a brown overcoat which was buttoned up. The top clothing was slightly pulled up, and she was naked from the waist down, apart from a sock on the left foot. The other sock was found a few yards behind her and a dress was found a few yards beyond that.

She was cold to touch. *Rigor mortis* was beginning to wear off. There was bruising and blood around the left side of the face. There were cuts to the palms of both hands. Both knees were severely abraded and there was pink discolouration. There was a bruise on the left hip. On pulling up the clothing several wounds were noticed in the right upper abdomen, to be described later. There was no obvious evidence of bruising or injury to the neck. There was no evidence of petechial haemorrhages in the eyes. There was some blood staining on opening the coat from the region of the abdomen. Car keys and a blood stained handkerchief were found in the right coat pocket. There was slight bruising and swelling to the left wrist—evidence of rheumatoid arthritis. Two articles of footwear apparently belonging to the deceased were noted placed at intervals between the copse and the road. There had been heavy rain within the previous 24 hours, but earlier that week it had been very cold and dry.

Dr Acland carried out his post-mortem examination at Shrewsbury's Copthorne hospital at 6.25 pm that same day. After removing Miss Murrell's clothes—many of which had holes in, presumably as a result of the knife attack— Dr Acland described the body:

The body—height 5′ 6½″ and weight, 109 lbs—was that of an elderly white woman. There was grey hair tied in a bun.

There were severe rheumatoid arthritic changes, particularly in the wrists and fingers with ulna deviation (this is a distortion of the hand). There was a slight swelling of the knees and lateral deviation of toes. *Rigor mortis* was wearing off. Hypostasis was faint in the right lateral position. There were large areas of abrasion of both knees and this showed pink discolouration. There

was no evidence of bruising or injuries to the scalp. On
the right side of the face was a diffuse bruise, over the
right forehead, around the right eye, across the right
cheek measuring 10 x 6 cm. There was a split in the skin
just below the right eye. The nature of this injury was
probably due to a broad blunt impact. This could be due
to the car accident, but equally likely due to kicking. It
is slightly less likely to be due to punching, although this
is still a possibility. It again is less likely due to falling
or stumbling.

There was a bruise to the left side of the chin measuring 3.5 cm diameter. Again, it is uncertain as to the
nature of this injury. It could be due to punching or
falling. There were two faint scratches to the left side
of the neck and a 1 cm diameter bruise to the mid-lower
neck just above the supraclavicular notch (this is the
mid-portion of the neck). Some dried blood was present
in the right ear. She had a cataract in the right eye. No
petechial haemorrhages were noted. The mouth appeared
uninjured. The upper jaw was edentulous (toothless).
The lower teeth appeared unremarkable. No other
injuries were noted to the head or neck externally. On
the anterior trunk there was a diffuse bruise over the
right shoulder and over the upper portion of the right
chest, measuring 12 x 10 cm. This corresponded to a
fracture of the clavicle (the collar bone) in the lateral
third of the clavicle. On the right arm 12 cm below the
point of the shoulder, in the region of the biceps muscle
was a penetrating incised wound measuring 2 x 0.8 cm.
This corresponded with a smaller incised wound on the
medial aspect measuring 0.5 cm. A probe showed communication between the two wounds, and hence a
penetrating wound had transfixed the arm at this point.
Just to the right of the midline between the umbilicus
and the line of the nipples was a superficial scratch
horizontal in nature measuring 4 cm long. In the region
of the right upper abdomen in the costal margin there
were a group of penetrating incised wounds.

The first was 3 cm away from the umbilicus and was
a small incised wound measuring 0.6 cm in length. 3 cm
beyond this were two adjacent wounds measuring 0.6
cm in length. 3 cm beyond this were two adjacent in-

cised wounds, the lateral wound measuring 1 cm and the medial wound measuring 1.2 cm in diameter. 1.6 cm beyond this was a further incised wound measuring 1.8 cm long. 2.5 cm beyond this was an incised wound measuring 0.5 cm long.

On reflection of the skin an area of haemorrhage was noticed over the right lower ribs. An incised wound was noted through the inferior border of the costal margin medially measuring 1.4 cm long. The anterior superior portion of the liver showed two incised wounds; the lower wound was medial and measured 0.7 cm in length, and penetrated 1.5 cm.

The higher incised wound associated with surrounding bruising measured approximately 0.9 cm in length and perforated approximately 2.5 cm. On dissection, two distinct points were noted at the deeper level, as though the penetrating instrument had moved in the wound. There was little free blood in the abdominal cavity measuring about 150 mls. In my opinion the wounds were disabling but not fatal. On the anterior portion of both knees were large areas of abrasions which were pink in colour. Just above the left area of abrasion medially were a few faint scratches. On the mid-portion of skin 14 cm above the lateral malleolus (the other part of the ankle) was a laceration 1 cm long. There were no other injuries to the anterior trunk. There were no injuries to the posterior trunk, but soiling by earth and debris was noted over the buttocks. The external genitalia appeared normal. There was a reddened poly-poid lesion at the external meatus (passage), with a naturally occurring phenomena. There was no evidence macroscopically of sexual assault.

The right hand showed rheumatoid arthritic changes with ulnar deviation. On the dorsum (back) of the right hand was an abrasion with partial avulsion (tearing away) of the skin at the base of the right thumb. There was bruising over the dorsum of the hand measuring 3 x 2 cm with faint splits in the skin. There was a bruise of 1 cm in diameter over the radial head and there was a diffuse bruise 4 cm diameter over the ulna 4 cm proximal to the wrist. On the ventral surface of the right hand was a 4 cm sharp shallow incision extending across the

palm of the thumb, then in continuation there was a
further incision extending across the palm from the
thumb, then in continuation there was a further incision
0.6 cm away at the base of the ring finger. This in my
opinion is consistent with a defensive wound, as though
grasping a sharp implement.

The left-hand dorsal surface—there was diffuse con-
gestion over the knuckles. There was a small superficial
nick in the webbing between the middle and ring
fingers about 0.3 cm long. There was a bruise on the
dorsal surface over the ulna head of 2 cm diameter and on
the ventral palm which again is consistent with a defensive
incised wound.

Dr Acland then made an internal examination, dissecting
Miss Murrell's body to see if there were any other damage.
He found that her heart and major blood vessels were
normal, as were her lungs—so too were her gall bladder
and apart from the wounds, her liver.

The stomach contained coffee ground material (blood
which is discoloured by the acid in the stomach). Numerous punctate erosions were noted in the mucosa and
this is a feature consistent with hypothermia. Although
it was perhaps contributory to the death, I don't think
she died of blood loss. There were about four or five
stab wounds in the lower abdomen, there was a penetrating wound to the upper arm, a fracture of the clavicle
(collar bone) and injuries to the face and neck.

There were also defence wounds to both hands. These
are typical injuries you would see in somebody who is
fighting off an attack from a sharp weapon. I think the
weapon was probably a knife. I can't confidently say
that it was a single or double bladed knife, but probably
more likely to be a single bladed knife.

It is possible that had she received medical treatment
immediately after the attack she would not have died.
I think that an elderly lady with some moderately serious
injuries, in very cold weather, would die of hypothermia
within five to ten hours. Had she received medical treatment within that period she may have survived.

Dr Acland then speculated on how Miss Murrell may have come to have been stabbed.

> I am cautious about drawing too many conclusions from the evidence we have had, but I think that from the evidence I saw, Miss Murrell may have been trying to escape from the car and was pursued and possibly frog-marched with an arm across her neck, and the knife held towards her.
> The injuries to the knees were I think due to her crawling around. It seems probable that any wounding that was done would be consistent with an attack whilst she was upright, but I can't rule out the fact that she may have fallen to the ground and then been kicked around the head or shoulder.
> A blood-stained handkerchief was found in the right pocket of her coat, which was adjacent to the stab wounds, but I am not sure whether the handkerchief was stained because of this, or whether she used the handkerchief to mop up some earlier injury. The evidence suggests she had been stabbed through her clothing.

Dr Acland then said he thought Miss Murrell's head wounds had most probably been caused by a kick. He thought it unlikely that she had been injured in her car as the vehicle was free of any blood-stains. Although Dr Acland had already put forward his own theory about how Miss Murrell was 'frog-marched' into the copse, he did admit that there was another way she could have got there:

> I wouldn't like to say whether the abrasions on the hands were consistent with crawling, or whether they were due to the assault.
> The abrasions on the knees could have been consistent with her being dragged. This is a possibility, but I did not notice any other abrasions to the wrists, legs or to the toes which you might expect if she was dragged. I can't exclude that she might have been dragged.

Dr Acland told me:

All the relevant information from my post-mortem report was read out at the inquest. I suppose the coroner feels that some information needs to be held back so that it can be put to a suspect in future. I wrote to *The Times* about Miss Murrell's murder because there was so much speculation that I was somehow party to a cover-up. It's absolute nonsense.

It is my professional judgement that the cause of death was hypothermia because I do not think Miss Murrell died from her wounds.

I'm firmly of the opinion that the body was not moved after death, although in a hypothetical case, if two people were involved in lifting her, it is possible. But I don't think that is what happened.

I certainly don't support the police in every case, but in this one I think they are right.[3]

As a result of Dr Acland's evidence, and that of Det. Chief Supt Cole, coroner Colonel David Crawford Clarke reached a decision:

It is clear that having driven her to Hunkington, at some point removing her from the car, or her getting out of the car, and the place in which she was subsequently found, he attacked her and caused the injuries which brought about her subsequent death. The only verdict that I can record in such a case is that the deceased was killed unlawfully.

That Miss Murrell was killed unlawfully is beyond doubt. Unfortunately several aspects of the evidence as it was presented to the inquest are not. Small, dotted traces of mucus are consistent with hypothermia, but they do not make hypothermia the *only* possible cause of death. I have attended many inquests where pathologists have detected punctate erosions in the mucosa and yet decided on a variety of causes of death, ranging from multiple injuries to natural causes. One expert I have consulted said the presence of punctate erosions in the mucosa would not *by itself* be sufficient grounds for concluding that hypothermia was the *only* cause of death. In due course, a second post-mortem examination was carried out on the body of Hilda

Murrell, intended to be for the benefit of anyone apprehend-
ed for her murder. The results of that second post-mortem
examination remain confidential.

What seems crystal clear is that Miss Murrell suffered
numerous stab wounds, including some on her hands as
she tried to defend herself. Her attacker was brutal and
merciless. And he is still free.

A Reporter's Tale

THE PLOT THICKENS

An unsolved inquiry is, by definition, a mystery. But I want
to make it clear from the outset that the central thrust of
the police theory about Miss Murrell's death — that she was
killed by a chance burglar, seeking cash — cannot be ruled
out. It is not impossible. There are however so many
questions about the Murrell murder which are still unanswered that it is not surprising new theories have been put
forward.

The first point to make is that the police are only human.
They are capable of making mistakes. It is possible there
are errors in the methods used by detectives hunting Miss
Murrell's killer and/or in the way police presented evidence
at the inquest and to reporters.

It is, of course, equally possible that some reporters may
have made mistakes, either through inaccuracies or through
misunderstanding the importance of some evidence, and
that these may have fuelled the so-called 'conspiracy
theories' about Miss Murrell's death. Several examples of
what might be called 'reporter error' spring immediately to
mind. The first concerns the police use of a hypnotist two
months after Miss Murrell was killed.

The use of a hypnotist may be unorthodox but it is not
in itself sinister. There is nothing to suggest that hypnosis
was used to make witnesses *forget* evidence rather than to
help them remember.

The use of a hypnotist was first reported in the *Shropshire Star* on 23 May 1984. It was not until December that
some national newspapers, only lately aware of Miss
Murrell's unsolved murder, revived the story to help suggest
a conspiracy angle to the killing.

Another example of 'reporter error' concerns the police
use of the FBI. This was also reported fully in the *Shropshire Star* at the time, only to be revived later by national
newspapers seeking to link Miss Murrell's death with
British Intelligence. The police use of a hypnotist and the
FBI can, I suggest, be safely dismissed as red-herrings. If
the police had anything to hide they would not have told
the *Shropshire Star*.

Other examples became clear after a BBC television 'Crimewatch' programme transmitted on 14 March 1985, nearly a year after the murder.

Police used the programme to re-enact their version of Miss Murrell's killing, to refute some of the allegations made against them, and to appeal for more information.

During January, February and March 1985 some newspapers and television programmes[1] claimed that the final draft of Miss Murrell's Sizewell paper had been stolen. Det. Chief Supt Cole produced it on 'Crimewatch' and said it had never been missing.

After the programme, an anonymous viewer telephoned the BBC and claimed that Miss Murrell had been murdered by a MI5 agent who subsequently committed suicide. The following day, some newspapers claimed police were following up this 'new' lead.[2] In fact, police were not following it up.

They had been aware of the claim for several weeks, knew the identity of the person who was making it and had dismissed the idea.

Nevertheless, there are some unanswered questions where police *have* been less than candid with reporters. A week after Miss Murrell was killed, police said that one of the witnesses had died while being interviewed by detectives. The cause of death was 'apparently' a heart attack but police could not be sure. They have refused to release any more information about the man to avoid distress to his family, even to the extent of refusing to confirm or deny the possibility that he might have been a suspect.

Relations between the West Mercia police and reporters deteriorated after a 'World in Action' documentary made by Granada TV in February 1985 and broadcast on 4 March.

The programme's producer, Stuart Prebble, says he was asked by police not to reveal the fact that the intruder at Miss Murrell's home had helped himself to a can of *Harp* lager. He says he was also asked not to reveal the fact that the killer seems to have attacked with a knife the passenger-side fascia panel of Miss Murrell's car and a grapefruit which was underneath it. Less than a fortnight later, the police themselves revealed this information on BBC TV's 'Crimewatch'. So if the information was confidential when the

'World in Action' programme was screened on 4 March, why was it suddenly in the public interest to broadcast it on 'Crimewatch' on 14 March?

Mr Prebble also asked if he could photograph the telephone wires at Miss Murrell's house which police said had been ripped from the wall. The police refused, says Mr Prebble, because the manner of telephone disconnection was also confidential. The BBC's 'Crimewatch' programme was actually allowed to broadcast what police said was a scene-of-crime video, showing clearly that the telephone wires had been ripped from the wall.

The 'World in Action' programme of 4 March reconstructed the murder and showed an actress dressed like Miss Murrell being frog-marched across the field in broad day-light to the copse where her body was later found. The 'Crimewatch' programme also re-constructed the murder, but instead showed that Miss Murrell may have attempted to run away from her attacker after the car slithered to a halt at Hunkington.

Journalistic vanity aside, there do seem to be serious discrepancies between the facilities afforded to the 'World in Action' programme-makers and the 'Crimewatch' programme which was made under police supervision. Perhaps this is because the West Mercia police felt they were being treated unfairly by 'World in Action'. The 'World in Action' interview with Assistant Chief Constable Bernard Drew had been very heavily edited to make him appear ignorant of some aspects of the killing. The pathologist, Dr Acland, also complained he had been 'set up' by 'World in Action'. Anyone who watched both the 'World in Action' documentary *and* the 'Crimewatch' programme will have been very confused as to what was going on.

The 'World in Action' programme explored the possibility that Miss Murrell's death might have been as a result of a conspiracy. The 'Crimewatch' programme ignored any suggestion of a conspiracy and allowed the police a free hand to put forward their own version of what happened.

The truth is probably that 'World in Action' tried too hard to establish a conspiracy angle and the 'Crimewatch' programme, by ignoring any such suggestion, was equally unbalanced.

The furious argument which followed both programmes

is testimony to the fact that journalists, like the police, are
very sensitive about criticism.

I want to concentrate now on some of the more obvious
reasons why Miss Murrell's murderer is still at large. One
of the earliest lessons learned by trainee detectives is the
need for extreme caution in issuing a description of anyone
wanted for questioning in an inquiry.

If the description is inaccurate, it is useless. In fact, it is
worse than useless because it wastes the time of both
police and public and makes it easier for the real criminal
to escape.

Yet consider the description of the man wanted for the
murder of Hilda Murrell, released by police just two days
after the beginning of the inquiry: 'aged about 30, 5ft 6in
to 5ft 7in tall, slim with fair hair.'

Ten days later police released a photo-fit picture of a
man with fair hair. But they also gave out a *new* description
which bore little resemblance to the first. Worse, it was
not much like the man in the photo-fit picture.

The later description said the killer was 'aged between
25 and 40, well-built and with broadish shoulders. He has
medium to dark brown collar-length hair, neatly groomed,
with a slight fringe. He is clean shaven and has a narrow
face and sallow complexion.'

Although this description is far more detailed than the
first, it must have confused some members of the public
who had earlier been told to look for a slim man with fair
hair.

At the same time, police said the killer was scruffily
dressed in either 'a grey suit or blue-grey jacket'. Detectives
themselves donned grey suits in an attempt to stir people's
memories.

Yet a month later Det. Chief Supt Cole began appealing
for information about a man wearing a blue anorak. What
was the purpose of having detectives run through the streets
in grey suits if the killer had been wearing a blue anorak?
Again, the public could easily have been confused.

Then police issued a new photo-fit picture and another
description. Instead of being 'slim with fair hair' or 'well-
built with medium to dark brown hair' the killer was now
thought to be 'of medium to large build with broad shoulders, with dark brown hair which may have been showing

traces of grey'. He was also thought to have 'deep set, dark eyes'.

Obviously you cannot blame the police if the public are slow in coming forward with information, but Det. Chief Supt Cole went out of his way to praise the public for their assistance. He repeatedly assured reporters he was pleased with the way the inquiry was progressing and was confident of an early arrest. 'We have made fantastic progress,' he said. 'We just need that little bit more information to bring it to a successful conclusion.'[3]

Despite the apparently conflicting descriptions and photofit pictures, police believe the information they have fits only one man — the killer. They have never considered the possibility that the reasons the descriptions seem so dissimilar is because they might refer to *two* men. This is a theory which assumes more significance later on.

Another essential ingredient in any murder story is the establishment of a motive. Police have insisted from the outset that the murderer was after cash and some form of sexual activity. They have based their assumption of the theft motive on the fact that the £50 Miss Murrell is known to have drawn from her bank could not be recovered. Is this really so surprising?

Miss Murrell had been shopping. No doubt part of her £50 was in the till at Safeways. She had also settled a small debt for some charity draw tickets. How much change would she have out of £50? I do not question that the killer may have taken some money, only why the police are so adamant that theft must be the prime motive. Would a common burglar have ignored the relatively easy pickings of Miss Murrell's small valuables, jewellery and pictures? The drawers and cupboards at her home had been gone through, in an orderly manner, and her papers rifled. If the murderer was a chance burglar he certainly did not behave like one. It is here that we come across one of the inconsistencies in the way police released information about the murder.

Det. Chief Supt Cole told the inquest that Miss Murrell's house had been 'thoroughly and systematically searched.' Yet nine months earlier he was quoted by reporters as saying the house had been 'ransacked', as if the killer was a common burglar who had left a typical mess.

Police visited the house on the Friday evening and twice on the Saturday morning and noticed nothing wrong.[4] Yet Hilda Murrell's gardener, David Williams, and her neighbour, Brian George, immediately detected signs of a burglary.[5] 'Any lay man would recognise instantly there was something wrong,' said Mr George. 'There was washing on the floor and seed packets around the place. We found a couple of handbags and general mail on the table in the scullery. There was three days' mail at the front part of the hall.'

When police arrived on Saturday at Miss Murrell's house for the third time, after the discovery of her body, they found her handbags, old and new, open on the kitchen table.[6] Had they not noticed these on their two previous visits? And if those handbags had been there when Miss Murrell returned from shopping, would she really have gone upstairs to change, as police believe? Would a common burglar have gone to the trouble of abducting an elderly, frail woman, in her own car, when it would have been so much easier simply to run away?

Police arriving at the house on the Saturday morning found a small pool of rainwater inside the back door.[7] How did it get there? Several witnesses say they saw police officers in uniform at Miss Murrell's house on the Friday night. This was later confirmed by Home Office minister Giles Shaw, who said a police constable 'saw signs of habitation and the back door unlocked, but did not search the house as he assumed that nothing was amiss, despite being unable to make contact with anybody there.' Nothing amiss? Det. Chief Supt Cole told the inquest that the curtains at Miss Murrell's home had been drawn since the Wednesday on which she was abducted and the light had been left on. Was this not thought odd, or was it not realised until later? It was known from Wednesday afternoon onward that Miss Murrell's car was in a ditch near Hunkington Moat. Why should a police officer visiting the house on Friday 'assume that nothing was amiss'?

On 26 March Det. Chief Supt Cole told reporters that the police had had to force an entry to gain access to Miss Murrell's home. How does this fit with Mr Shaw's statement to Parliament that police on Friday found the door unlocked? Why did police visit the house again early on

Saturday morning—the day the body was found—and still notice nothing wrong?

Police told reporters early on[8] that Miss Murrell was subjected to some form of sexual activity but decline to say exactly what 'for operational reasons'. Det. Chief Supt Cole told reporters in April that 'forensic tests have established Miss Murrell was sexually assaulted, although there was no evidence of rape.' Police say reporters have misconstrued the information as contradictory, but admit that 'some confusion has occurred over two police press releases.

'In answer to a direct question, had she been raped, the police replied no, but did later say that the deceased had been subjected to some form of sexual activity. Both these statements are true and are not contradictory.'

Police continued: 'The evidence indicates what in legal terms could be construed as a sexual assault. It is not intended that any further details on this particular aspect will be released for two reasons—(a) to ensure no further distress is caused to Miss Murrell's family and (b) operational reasons concerning future interviews.' On 25 January 1985 the *New Statesman* reported that a man who is an accredited counsellor to people with sexual problems was visited by police *before* Miss Murrell's body was discovered and asked if he knew of anyone fitting the description of a loner who might break into women's bedrooms and be violent. It was not until 14 March 1985 that Det. Chief Supt Cole confirmed that the 'sexual activity' had been an act of masturbation in Miss Murrell's bedroom, and that the forensic tests had established the presence of semen on Miss Murrell's clothes.[9]

But the manner in which police released some information and then refused to release sufficient explanation about it succeeded only in confusing the public to which they were appealing for help.

Catching murderers is not easy and the police are the people trained and paid to do it best. Nevertheless, police can and do make mistakes and the evidence I have presented here is intended to suggest that the failure to catch Hilda Murrell's killer could be as much due to the 'cock-up' theory as anything else. There is, however, other evidence which lends weight to a conspiracy theory.

As an active peace and anti-nuclear campaigner, Hilda

C

Murrell will have been known to the nearest thing in
Britain to a secret, political police force, the Special Branch.

The Special Branch have an office in Shrewsbury where
they will have collected information on anyone they
believed to be 'subversive'. Incredibly, a 78-year-old ex-
rose grower will have fitted into that category, so widely
drawn is the definition of 'subversive'.

There is some evidence that Miss Murrell was under
active surveillance (phone tapping and mail interception).
It is almost certain that the Special Branch will have had a
file on her political activities, as they do on thousands of
ordinary citizens. This is not paranoia, it is fact. It is also a
fact that officers from the Special Branch were involved at
an early stage in the inquiry into Hilda Murrell's murder.

Whether they were involved in a 'fishing expedition' to
gather more information on the peace and environment
groups to which Hilda Murrell belonged, or whether their
involvement was even more sinister—such as to ensure that
no one was ever caught—is not known.

Giles Shaw confirmed the involvement of the Special
Branch in the House of Commons on 19 December 1984.
'It should be understood that specialist officers are often
called upon to perform non-specialist roles when the man-
power demands are great. This has been the situation in this
case and Special Branch officers have been used on the
routine murder inquiry work.'

The 'routine' work included an investigation of Miss
Murrell's connections with the anti-nuclear movement. The
secretary of the Nuclear Weapons Freeze Advertising Campaign, Richard Wiggs, is one such connection. He lives at
Biggleswade in Bedfordshire and never met Hilda Murrell,
although they corresponded for 20 years. 'A few days after
she was killed,' said Mr Wiggs, 'I was telephoned by my
bank, which had been telephoned by the Murder Inquiry
Room at Shrewsbury.

'The bank asked whether I was willing for my number to
be given to the police, who wished to ask me about Hilda
Murrell. I agreed to this, and soon after was telephoned by
a detective who said that the investigators were trying to
contact all the organisations with which Miss Murrell had
connections.

'They were led to me because she had made contributions by bankers' order to the Nuclear Weapons Freeze Advertising Campaign.

'The detective asked how long I had known Miss Murrell, how well I knew her, whether we had ever met, whether we had been in contact recently. In July I was telephoned again — they were still trying to trace *New Perspective Publishers Ltd*, to whom Miss Murrell had sent a cheque for £15.'[10]

Mr Wiggs is not the only one who thinks this was an extraordinary effort by the police if they were really only seeking 'an ordinary burglar'.

Special Branch officers 'were used,' the police said, 'because it was felt that their experience particularly fitted them to deal with this inquiry.'[11]

Nevertheless, the theory that the police were never meant to catch Hilda Murrell's killer developed when it was learned that three of the officers involved in the hunt were playing golf at a time when they should have been playing detectives. They skived off work, the theory goes, because they knew their senior officers did not want the killer caught. The police immediately and emphatically denied the suggestion: 'This is very far from true,' they said. 'Senior officers on the murder inquiry carrying out their supervisory duties became aware of discrepancies in these officers' duties and reported it to the Deputy Chief Constable, who implemented disciplinary procedures and caused them to be suspended.'

The next apparently suspicious piece of evidence concerns the state of Miss Murrell's telephone when police arrived at her house on the Saturday morning. They told reporters at the time that the wires had been ripped out of their wall socket. Police said nothing about the fact that people trying to telephone Miss Murrell, far from hearing an 'unobtainable' tone, heard a normal ringing tone as if there were nothing wrong.

The police could not have done more to fuel the conspiracy theory if they tried.

A British Telecom engineer told the London *Standard* on 7 February 1985 that the telephone had indeed been disabled, but by someone with an above-average knowledge of how to go about it.

The junction-box connecting the cord from the telephone to the wall was found with one screw loosened and one of the four wires—only one, coloured green—had been *unscrewed* and disconnected.

The green wire governs the telephone bell. This means the telephone was still working. It also means the security services could use the telephone mouthpiece as a 'bug' to listen to what was going on in the room. The only thing about the telephone which was not working was the bell, yet police continued to insist that this did not constitute a sophisticated manner of tampering with a phone.

Miss Murrell's neighbour, Brian George, who was one of the first people to enter the house on the Saturday morning, is another witness who thought the telephone had been disconnected by a professional.[12]

The telephone at Miss Murrell's 'shack' at Llanymynech was also out of order on the day of the murder, although police said nothing about it at the time. In the early weeks of the inquiry police said they could not discuss the manner of telephone disconnection 'for operational reasons' but issued a statement saying the phone at Miss Murrell's home had been 'rendered partly inoperative' and could still be used to ring out—which is some way from having its wires ripped from the wall socket. Eventually, a year after the killing, police said the telephone which could still be used was an upstairs extension. They showed a video of a telephone whose wires had been ripped from the wall and said it had been recorded in Miss Murrell's home over the weekend on which the body was discovered. This means either that Mr George and the BT engineer are mistaken, or the wires had been ripped from the wall later. Police said the Llanymynech telephone malfunctioned due to a capacitor fault caused by storm damage. There is no record of any electrical storm in the Oswestry area during February or March 1984.

A friend of Miss Murrell's, Michael Gilmore, claims he actually used the Llanymynech telephone on 23 February, when it worked perfectly.[13]

British Telecom is supposed to keep a house card on file with details of all telephones in any given area. The file on Miss Murrell's Shrewsbury home is kept at the BT depot at Ditherington. It carries no reference to either the damage caused by the burglary or the subsequent police investigation of the phone, despite police assurances that both the Llany- mynech and Shrewsbury telephones' faults were 'independently assessed by a BT engineer'.[14]

We come now to the most puzzling aspect of the police inquiry. Why was it that Miss Murrell was abducted on Wednesday but her body not found until Saturday?

A local farmer, Ian Scott, went walking through the very copse where Miss Murrell's body was later found at 3.30 pm on the Thursday afternoon. He was counting trees with a view to felling and obviously studied them carefully. He is an experienced countryman and has a keen eye. He is absolutely certain that if Miss Murrell's body had been at Hunkington Moat on Thursday afternoon he would have seen it. Mr Scott says he studied the copse so carefully he would have fallen over Miss Murrell's body if it had been there. 'I would have seen a dead rabbit, let alone a dead woman,' he said.[15]

On the actual day of the murder, two boys stole the tax disc from Miss Murrell's Renault. They subsequently burned it when they heard she had been murdered. Their case was dealt with on 18 April, but it is not known how the police discovered the theft, or if the boys were questioned to find out if they had seen anything.[16]

At about 4.30 pm on Thursday, a tractor driver working in a field near to the spot where Miss Murrell's body was found saw a man in a big dark car stop on the road, walk across the field to the copse, then return 15 to 20 minutes later, before driving off. Local people claim to have seen lights moving in the copse on the Thursday evening.[17] Det. Chief Supt Cole told the inquest that Miss Murrell's car was reported to police on the Wednesday afternoon. A police statement issued later said: 'Miss Murrell's Renault car was seen in the ditch at Hunkington on 21 March by a local farmer who notified an off-duty police officer at 5.20 pm. Officers went to the scene within an hour but there were no apparent suspicious circumstances. The officers made a preliminary search of the immediate area but took no further action at that stage.'

Was the search made by the officers inefficient, or was there another reason why they could not see Miss Murrell's body, supposedly only 500 yards away?

As I said at the outset of this chapter, police can make mistakes. Det. Chief Supt Cole told the inquest he arrived at the scene where Miss Murrell's body was found at 1.30 pm on Saturday. The Home Office pathologist, Dr Peter Acland, told the inquest *he* was called to go to the scene by Mr Cole two hours earlier—but this is a minor inconsistency. Dr Acland, however, did tell the inquest he could not rule out the possibility that the marks on Miss Murrell's body meant she had been dragged to the spot where she was later found. This might explain the wide spread of her clothing.

So why did it take three days to find the body of Hilda Murrell? Could this be, as Sherlock Holmes once said, the case of the dog that did not bark in the night? That the body was not found for the simple reason that it was not there?

The Sizewell Connection

A few weeks before she was murdered, Hilda Murrell telephoned her friends Gerard and Fern Morgan-Grenville. She wanted to discuss her Sizewell paper and was in a state of some agitation. Her parting words on the telephone were: 'If they don't get me first, I want the world to know that one old woman has seen through their lies.'

Mr Morgan Grenville remembers the telephone conversation clearly. 'I was in the bath at the time,' he said. 'My wife answered the telephone and established that it was Hilda, and then came to me and said that Hilda seemed especially anxious to talk to me. I spoke to her for something like 30 minutes.'

Mr Morgan-Grenville told me: 'I remember the telephone conversation so clearly because it was February and quite cold. I wouldn't normally sit there shivering in my bathrobe to talk to someone on the telephone — I'd call them back. But Hilda seemed especially anxious. We discussed her Sizewell paper and other things connected with politics — she wondered how long the present Government was likely to be in for — and the conversation lasted for about half-an-hour. I was frozen stiff by the time we finished.'[1]

Fern Morgan-Grenville recalls: 'Hilda did sound very worried when I answered the telephone. I cannot think why, I can't put my finger on it exactly; but whatever it was it made me call my husband from the bathroom. There was no question of saying "He'll call you back" — she did sound somewhat uncharacteristically upset.'[2]

The Morgan-Grenvilles have a thick file of correspondence on Hilda Murrell's anti-nuclear paper. The police have never asked to see it.

Miss Murrell was the epitome of a confident, sensible, English countrywoman and not given to wild imaginings. Yet like many people who hold somewhat radical views, she thought she might be in danger from people who disagreed with her. In particular, she thought her opposition to nuclear power might make her a target. Miss Murrell had just completed a 16-page document which she planned to present at the Sizewell B public inquiry as a comment from 'an ordinary citizen'.

Her paper said the waste from nuclear power stations was 'the worst form of industrial pollution ever created by man. Even a desperate need for energy would not justify creating the worst of all pollutants.' Mr Morgan-Grenville shared her views. 'I think her paper was a remarkable one because she had spent her life growing roses and was held in great esteem as being an exceptionally intelligent person,' he said. 'She only started to study nuclear physics well into her retirement. And for one person to see so transparently what was going on in that industry, and what is still going on, was truly remarkable.'

The Sizewell B public inquiry was held at the Snape Maltings in Suffolk and lasted more than two years, drawing to a close in March 1985. Chaired by Sir Frank Layfield, its remit was to study the proposals of the Central Electricity Generating Board (CEGB) to build a pressurised water reactor (PWR) nuclear power station on the site of an existing power station on the coast at Sizewell.

At the time of writing, Sir Frank has yet to make his report, but several aspects of the 26-month-long inquiry are worthy of mention. The arguments advanced against the PWR were many and varied, but most were based on the need to conserve the natural environment. Hilda Murrell took a close interest in the inquiry's progress.

The objectors in whose company Miss Murrell found herself included an Australian aborigine who wanted to complain about how uranium mining was destroying his homeland; Dr Ross Hesketh, a former CEGB scientist who said the plutonium produced by the reactor process could be used in nuclear weapons and the chairman of the Conservative Party, John Gummer, who feared an unacceptable increase in lorry traffic along narrow country lanes.

The Suffolk Preservation Society claimed the coastal site selected by the CEGB was an area of outstanding natural beauty and should not be damaged by further building. Organisations like the Town and Country Planning Association and the Council for the Protection of Rural England put forward economic arguments designed to show that nuclear power was unnecessary. Observers at the inquiry said later that the CEGB seemed at its weakest when talking about the disposal of radioactive waste which would be produced if the Sizewell B project went ahead. It was this particular aspect of the inquiry which most concerned Hilda Murrell, although of course she had much in common with many of those objecting on other grounds.

The CEGB was forced to admit during questioning that the disposal of radioactive waste was still an unknown factor. Would it be stored at Sizewell or transported to the reprocessing plant at Sellafield in Cumbria? The absence of anywhere safe to dump the waste continues to pose a major problem for the nuclear industry.

The PWR uses ordinary 'light' water to cool its uranium fuel instead of the carbon dioxide gas hitherto used in British nuclear power stations. The design submitted for the inquiry's consideration was prepared by the American company, the Westinghouse Corporation.

The Westinghouse design is similar to the type of nuclear power station which in 1979 went out of control at Three Mile Island, near Pennsylvania in the United States. A leak of the cooling fluid brought the reactor close to melting down and led to a discharge of radioactive iodine gas into the atmosphere. The surrounding area had to be evacuated and some anti-nuclear protestors have claimed the incident as the worst accident in the history of atomic power.

As a result of the Three Mile Island accident, the United States nuclear authorities have lost faith in the PWR design and have stopped building them. Perhaps more than any other interested party, the Westinghouse Corporation has much to lose if the Sizewell B PWR is never built. On 8 March 1985, as the public inquiry drew to a close, *The New Statesman* described Westinghouse as 'paranoid'. Hilda Murrell argued eloquently against the Sizewell project:

> The inescapable burden now inflicted on posterity, imposes a straight moral choice, which was not faced in the beginning but which must be faced now. Even a desperate need for energy would not justify creating these worst of all pollutants whose control for merely a few centuries (in the case of high-level waste) we cannot guarantee, far less that of the long-lived actinides which are forever.
>
> We have not even a moderate need for this technology, never mind a desperate one. This is a failed and dying

industry, which is a major liability and should be closed down. The fact that plans can be made for adding to it shows an unbelievable degree of irresponsibility and stupidity in all concerned.

The Ordinary Citizen implores the Inspector to urge the right moral choice on the government, which should re-direct all its spare billions towards energy conservation, cleaning up fossil-fuelled power stations, and developing alternative energy sources.[3]

The possibility that Miss Murrell's death might be connected with her anti-nuclear views was first explored publicly by journalist Judith Cook in *The New Statesman* on 9 November 1984. Although police instantly dismissed the idea, it would not go away.

On 2 December a headline in *The Observer* read: 'Silkwood Parallels in English Woman's Death'. The report suggested that Miss Murrell might have been killed because she was 'too much of a nuisance' to the nuclear industry and made a comparison with another unsolved death. 'The Murrell case,' said *The Observer*, 'which has proved particularly baffling for police, has striking parallels with that of Karen Silkwood, the young American who died in a mysterious car crash 10 years ago. Karen, whose story was later made into a film "Silkwood" starring Meryl Streep, was an analyst at a nuclear fuel processing plant in Oklahoma.'

The Observer continued: 'She was on her way to a meeting with a journalist to give details of contamination and alleged cover-ups at the factory but was found dead at the wheel of her crashed car. There were allegations that Karen had been murdered in order to silence her. Papers she had with her in the car were missing.

'The FBI investigated the death but came up with no firm evidence, though they did discover traces of plutonium in Karen's body.'

The theory that Miss Murrell was killed because of her anti-nuclear views, or because she 'knew too much' about the Sizewell B project, has been widely held by her friends and relatives ever since the murder. Miss Murrell had a note in her diary to discuss her paper with friends, Diana Gold from Shrewsbury and Helen Paling-Wright, a nuclear physic-

ist who lives near Miss Murrell's Llanymynech 'shack'. Miss
Murrell was killed before she could keep the appointments.[4]
The initial police response was to dismiss the nuclear theory
as utter rubbish. Police also denied suggestions that the
Special Branch were involved in the murder hunt. As we
know, the police later had to correct both statements and
admit that they had in fact employed the Special Branch on
an investigation of the Sizewell Connection.

Police maintained from the outset that the only thing
stolen from Miss Murrell's house was a small amount of
cash. But several of Miss Murrell's friends believed the final
draft of her Sizewell paper was also missing.

Although the typed version of the document was found,
it is known that Miss Murrell was still working on her paper
and trying to improve it. The day before she was abducted,
she wrote in her diary: 'Started polishing and correcting
paper. Eliminated 16 lines from first six pages. Not enough
though.[5]

It is unlikely that, in the time available to her, Miss
Murrell could have substantially changed her Sizewell document from the version which was in fact presented on her
behalf to the inquiry in September 1984. But the fact that
her 'polished and corrected' paper was thought to be
missing added to the mystery.

The two boys who stole Miss Murrell's tax disc from her
car on the supposed day of the murder say there were
papers on the back seat. Police found nothing.[6]

It was not until a year after the murder that Det. Chief
Supt Cole revealed that the 'missing' document had been in
police hands all the time.[7]

Supporters of the Sizewell Connection theory were
encouraged in their speculation by a major report in *The
Observer* on 27 January 1985, which revealed that objectors
to the Sizewell B project were indeed the target of secret
surveillance.

As I cannot improve on *The Observer's* report, nor add
to its importance, I reproduce it here in full:

Objectors at the public inquiry into the Sizewell nuclear
reactor have been the target of a secret surveillance
operation by a private detective agency which has links
with British Intelligence.

The objectors include major environmental pressure groups, the peace movement, the anti-nuclear lobby and local residents. Without their knowledge, names and home addresses and political leanings, as well as links with the media, were gathered by private detectives sub-contracted by Zeus Security Consultants, which is run by former military intelligence officer, Mr Peter Hamilton.

Mr Hamilton yesterday declined to name who had commissioned the operation from him, saying only that it was a 'private client'.

Zeus used local agents who set up dummy peace groups and posed as conservationists to gather information.

The disclosure of the operation — in documents obtained by *The Observer* is likely to cause a furore in Parliament and could even damage the prospects for the Sizewell inquiry, which has lasted two years.

The revelation that private investigators were monitoring the objectors may influence the police inquiry into the mysterious death of anti-nuclear campaigner Hilda Murrell, although there is no suggestion that Mr Hamilton's operation was involved. Police were previously unaware that private investigators had been involved at Sizewell and may wish to see if they have any background information to offer.

Miss Murrell, aged 78, was one of the Sizewell objectors. She was due to give evidence at the hearings, but last March she was found dead in woods outside Shrewsbury, where she lived. She had disturbed an intruder in her home and been abducted and killed.

The possibility that her death was connected with Sizewell grew last week with the disclosure by Harlech television that the only item missing from her home after the burglary was the final draft of her Sizewell paper.

The investigation of the Sizewell objectors was mounted by Mr Hamilton, a member of the Institute of Professional Investigators, who claims he has spent most of his life 'in the security and intelligence world'.

Mr Hamilton has been outspoken in warning of the threat of 'domestic subversion' in trade unions. Official company documents say the job of Zeus is 'to provide security services of all kinds to Government and other authorities'.

In January 1983, as the public hearings into the planned £1.2 billion power station opened, Mr Hamilton was hired to monitor the objectors. He passed the work, through another member of the Institute, to a company in Colchester called Contingency Services run by Mr Vic Norris, who is not himself an IPI member. The purpose of the exercise was spelled out in an internal briefing sheet: 'Client wishes to ascertain identities of principal objectors at the Sizewell atomic power station at Snape Maltings. If possible, obtain list of objectors, their connections with media, political leanings etc'.

Mr Norris promotes himself as a specialist in 'delicate work'. He claims to have worked for the Government. 'We have a couple of very good imitation lefties,' he told a potential client last week. 'They know the score. They know the patois that these people use. They can drop names. They have got connections. We can infiltrate all right. I do the work that the Home Office don't want their own people to do'.

Mr Norris started work on 21 January 1983 by contacting a local journalist, posing as a sympathiser with the objectors. On 25 January, he passed on the names of five pressure groups who were involved in the hearings: the Town and Country Planning Association, the East Anglian Alliance, Friends of the Earth, Greenpeace and CND.

On 27 January he filed a report which accurately listed 16 groups who were particularly active among the 164 objectors. He commented that some of the groups appeared to have economic or conservationist motives, adding: 'Some of the others are openly political and there are clear indications of co-operation between some of these political groups'. Mr Norris claimed that Friends of the Earth shared offices in London 'with a number of organisations of the extreme left'. He described freelance consultant Graham Searle as 'a professional protestor' and claimed that the Greenpeace campaigns director Pete Wilkinson was masquerading as a local resident.

He went on to order searches into the financial records of Greenpeace and Friends of the Earth and noted that it was hoped that this would yield the home address of Mr Searle — one of the founders of Friends of the Earth.

Posing as an objector with the name of Page, one of Mr Norris's assistants approached the documents officer at the inquiry, Jerry Crowe, and obtained a three-page list of objectors, giving the names and addresses of 27 people, including trade unionists, county councillors and members of the Labour Party.

In his reports he claims to have established three 'dummy peace groups' which had made contact with genuine peace activists and had been accepted as 'bona fide'. He suggested that they would be a useful tool to discredit CND and 'put a stopper' on the organisation's work.

The Observer has no evidence that the surveillance operation at Sizewell is linked with the death of Miss Murrell. The Special Branch have already investigated allegations by Miss Murrell's friends that she died because of her Sizewell activity, and have ruled out the connection.

West Mercia police said yesterday that the Special Branch inquiry had failed to yield any information on the activity of private detectives. 'We are quite prepared to look into it,' a spokesman said.

Mr Hamilton yesterday confirmed that he had organised the Sizewell operation. Initially he suggested that it had been mounted to find 'subversives who were agitating'. Later he said he had been working for a private client who believed that information had leaked to some of the objectors. 'I can absolutely assure you that this had nothing to do with Whitehall,' he said. Mr Norris declined to comment on *The Observer* report.

The Observer's story was—and still is—deeply disturbing. It subsequently became known that Zeus Security Consultants did not pass the contract directly to Vic Norris's Contingency Services. Instead Zeus approached the Sapphire Investigations Bureau, in Acle, Norfolk, which was run by private detective Barrie Peachman.[8] Shortly after Miss Murrell's murder, Barrie Peachman seems to have shot himself—but not before he had passed on the Zeus contract to spy on Sizewell objectors to Mr Norris. The inquest into Mr Peachman's death recorded a verdict of suicide after evidence that he was emotionally involved with a woman

who worked for him. An anonymous caller to BBC TV's
'Crimewatch' on 14 March 1985, who claimed to work for
MI5, alleged that Mr Peachman was Miss Murrell's murderer.
Police dismissed the claim as nonsense.

Vic Norris has a quite amazing background. He has been
featured twice in the *News of the World* in recent years
because of his satanist activities. At one time he ran his own
Anglian Satanic Church. Mr Norris is also an enthusiastic
fascist, having run two extreme Right-wing groups of his own —
the 5000 Group and the Salvo Society. He also runs AH
Services, which is named after Adolf Hitler and markets nazi
regalia. Mr Norris was jailed for six years in 1969 for a long
list of child sex offences.[9]

Needless to say, the involvement of a bizarre character
such as Mr Norris contributes greatly to the theory that
Miss Murrell could have been killed by someone looking
for information related to the Sizewell inquiry. If Miss
Murrell's murder was an irrational act, without motive,
then the police should perhaps be looking more closely at
cranky organisations which might have been spying on her.
As Mr Hamilton told *The Observer*, the private detectives
were brought in by a client who believed information had
leaked to some of the objectors.

The identity of the client is known only to Mr Hamilton,
who is not saying. The kind of information which could
have been leaked is also a mystery, as there is little which
is not known about the type of nuclear reactor proposed
at Sizewell. All we know for certain is that whatever the
information was, it was sufficiently sensitive for someone
to hire a private detective agency to stem the leak.

Mr Hamilton's own background as a military intelligence
officer, and the claims by Mr Norris that he undertakes
'delicate work' for the Government, doing jobs 'the Home
Office don't want their own people to do', begs some
serious questions about the way the security services operate. MI5 itself has a sub-section known as A1A, Technical
Operations, which works closely with the Special Branch
to gather information about people it regards as subversive.
This can involve the unofficial sub-contracting of some
intelligence work to private companies.

A1A, Technical Operations is responsible for carrying
out break-ins at the homes of Intelligence targets. Officers

then search for information and sometimes place an electronic eavesdropping device in a suitably discreet place.

Telephone tapping has reached epidemic proportions, despite official denials. As the journalist Duncan Campbell has demonstrated clearly, the security services now have the capacity simultaneously to intercept telephone messages at several thousand homes. The Government has for many years maintained that only a few hundred telephones are tapped at any one time. A former MI5 officer with 14 years' experience, Cathy Massiter, has confirmed that MI5 collects information on thousands of CND supporters and others associated with the peace movement. She says MI5's operations 'expanded enormously' in the 1970s to include spying on solicitors, barristers, journalists and pressure groups. It had for years been spying on active trade unionists.

Ms Massiter's revelations, included in a television programme[10] (whose transmission was delayed because of fears by the Independent Broadcasting Authority that it contravened the Official Secrets Act) support the earlier allegations of another former MI5 official, Michael Bettaney. Mr Bettaney is now in prison for trying to pass secrets to the KGB!

It is impossible to know exactly what we should make of all this in so far as it relates to the murder of Hilda Murrell. If we stick only to what we know, then we can say safely that what is normal behaviour for the security services is for most people so bizarre and illogical that it is *possible* they would be daft enough to search Miss Murrell's home for information related to the Sizewell inquiry.

By the same token, *as far as we know*, Miss Murrell did not have any information which posed any particular new threat to the nuclear industry or its supporters. It is, of course, possible that the same security services might want to search her home for another type of information — information related to something which for many had already established itself as one of the worst political scandals of the twentieth century.

The Belgrano Connection

DEEP-THROATS CLAIM THE MURDER WAS TO COVER UP A WAR-CRIME

On 3 April 1982 a special Saturday sitting of the House of Commons agreed to send a task force to the South Atlantic to recapture the Falkland Islands, which a few days earlier had been invaded by Argentina. Most MPs thought and certainly hoped that a diplomatic solution to the problem could still be found without any further loss of life. One Argentine soldier had been killed when the islands were invaded.

On 30 April, at Chequers, Mrs Thatcher and her war cabinet agreed to change the rules of engagement to allow the Argentine cruiser *General Belgrano* to be attacked outside Britain's declared 'total exclusion zone' while it was heading for home, away from the Falklands. The order to sink the *Belgrano* was sent from Chequers, via the Fleet headquarters at Northwood, to the nuclear-powered submarine HMS *Conqueror*.

On 2 May *Conqueror* carried out her orders, the *Belgrano* was sunk and 368 Argentine conscripts drowned. The rest is history—or is it?

One person who knew full details of Mrs Thatcher's message to HMS *Conqueror* was Lieutenant Commander Rob Green. He was an Intelligence officer at Northwood. He was also an active member of the Liberal Party. He viewed with alarm Mrs Thatcher's enthusiasm for a real shooting war. When the conflict was over, he resigned from the Navy. Miss Hilda Murrell was Rob Green's aunt. He visited her frequently and they shared many common interests. Rob Green never discussed with Miss Murrell any aspects of his role in the sinking of the *Belgrano* and has observed to the letter all his obligations under the Official Secrets Act.

Nevertheless, he says it is 'natural' that he would have come under suspicion as a potential leaker of information to the Labour MP, Tam Dalyell, whose campaign of Parliamentary questions continues to embarrass ministers.[1]

Rob Green presented his aunt's paper on nuclear power at the Sizewell inquiry in September 1984. He shared the views of his aunt's friends—that her murder might be connected with her involvement in the anti-nuclear movement.

D

'I am led to one solution only—that the break-in was to look for information, rather than valuables,' he said. 'I have a series of questions I want to ask about the police handling of the case, particularly their view of the proposition that the intruder—because he had no authority to kill her—had no alternative but to abduct her. Later that night he may have returned, put on the lights and drawn the curtains to make it look like an attempted burglary. He also left evidence to suggest a sex angle.'[2]

But on 19 December 1984 Mr Dalyell raised a different angle: he told the House of Commons he could not complain if Lt.-Commander Green had been under suspicion of leaking information about the *Belgrano*. 'He was one of the very few to have left the service, although I understand that he had decided to go before the Falklands crisis blew up,' he said.

Tam Dalyell continued:

Because Commander Green was known to have been unhappy about certain aspects of the Falklands war and was known to have wanted to leave the Navy, he came under a cloud of suspicion, wrongly, to the best of my knowledge, but certainly under a cloud of suspicion. It was thought that he might have copies of documents and raw signals that incriminated the Prime Minister, some of the originals of which had been destroyed on instructions from a very high level by the intelligence services.

Just as those of us who have had certain documents have taken the precaution of keeping them in friends' or relatives' houses while we have them, so it was thought that some of Rob Green's supposed records might be in the home of the aunt to whom he was close.[3]

The signals to which Rob Green had access were certainly embarrassing to the Prime Minister. They concerned not only the decision to sink the *Belgrano*, but signals from the South Atlantic patrol vessel HMS *Endurance* towards the end of 1981. *Endurance* sent an urgent message to Fleet HQ at Northwood reporting an apparent build-up of Argentine military strength which might constitute a threat to the Falkland Islands. Mrs Thatcher, and her defence secretary John Nott, ignored the signal. They thought it was

simply a piece of Royal Navy propaganda to save the
Endurance from being withdrawn from the South Atlantic.
In the event *Endurance* was withdrawn and the Argentine
government ordered an invasion of the Falklands.

For many, however, the sinking of the *Belgrano* was the
one single act which moved the Falklands' war from second
gear to fifth gear. They regard the act as an horrific war
crime.

Tam Dalyell told the Commons:

> Commander Green was, I am told, the person who physic-
> ally sent the signal to *Conqueror* that sank the *Belgrano*.
> I understand from his friends that he was also responsible
> for passing signals from *Endurance* which had shown
> beyond any reasonable doubt that an invasion of the
> Falklands was likely to happen.
>
> He considered the Falklands to be an unnecessary war,
> and the *Belgrano* sinking appalled him — albeit he judged
> it to be an unfortunate necessity — as did some other
> senior officers of the senior service. He took early retire-
> ment after 20 years in the Navy and left. From this Prime
> Minister and her colleagues he would come under suspic-
> ion. It is from the head of our security services that
> Parliament should be demanding an explanation, because
> of one thing I am certain — that there are persons in
> Westminster and Whitehall who know a great deal more
> about the violent death of Miss Hilda Murrell than they
> have so far been prepared to divulge.[4]

Rob Green says he appreciates Mr Dalyell's interest but
denies he sent the crucial signal. He does not believe Miss
Murrell's murder was related in any way to the sinking of
the *Belgrano*:

> I was one of a relatively small number of people who
> knew about the operation, but I find it hard that my
> aunt should have been investigated like that, although I
> would have expected myself to be.
>
> I certainly did not leave any documents for my aunt;
> I certainly would not have done anything so irrespons-
> ible and so stupid.
>
> I was too fond of Hilda to expose her to a risk like

that. But I did feel, on reading what Tam Dalyell had said, that he wouldn't have gone to all that trouble without justification. I have tried to remain objective throughout this unpleasant affair, so I feel I have a responsibility to look at his claim and to consider it.[5]

Tam Dalyell also told the House of Commons:

I am . . . given to understand—and I am happy to accept it—that there was no premeditated intention of doing away with Miss Murrell—only a search of her house when she was out. Alas, on Wednesday 21 March she returned unexpectedly to change. The intruders either arrived while she was dressing, or were disturbed by her.

Being a lady of courage and spunk, often found in that generation of women, Miss Murrell fought them. They too had to fight. They injured her and panicked.

I am informed that the intruders were not after money or nuclear information, but were checking the house to see it there were any *Belgrano*-related documents of Commander Green in the home of his aunt.

Things went disastrously wrong. They had no intention of injuring, let alone killing, a 78-year-old ex-rose grower. Yet, being the lady she was and in her home, Hilda Murrell fought and was severely injured. She was then killed or left to die from hypothermia, and the cover-up had to begin, because I am informed that the searchers were men of the British Intelligence.[6]

The following day the newspapers were awash with reports of Mr Dalyell's sensational claim. Police issued a statement saying :

. . . inquiries to date reveal no evidence to suggest the involvement of British Intelligence officers in this murder, nor has there been any approach whatsoever to the police from any agency to engage in a 'cover up' of the facts.

Arrangements have been made for senior detectives to interview Mr Dalyell . . . concerning his allegations. Any information he has concerning this inquiry will be analysed and acted upon accordingly.

Mr Dalyell's allegation seemed to confuse officials. Nine days later, Home Office minister Giles Shaw, having promised a 'proper and comprehensive reply,' simply dismissed Mr Dalyell's claim as complete nonsense:

> I am now able to state unreservedly that your allegations about the Intelligence services being involved are totally without foundation.[7]

The most interesting aspect of Mr Shaw's answer to Mr Dalyell is that it was made before the police had even begun their investigation into his claim that British Intelligence officers had been at Miss Murrell's house. How did Mr Shaw know that what he was saying was accurate? The police can not have told him.

Det. Supt Barry Maine, who was by this time in charge of the murder hunt, said he did not know if Mr Dalyell's claims were true or not and would continue to keep an open mind. He agreed there had been some anomalies in the way police had hitherto released information about the killing.[8]

Mr Dalyell's response to Mr Shaw caused few surprises:

> This is just typical of the whole *Belgrano* saga. Claims are dismissed before they have been properly considered and then sooner or later, lo and behold, the claims turn out to be true.
>
> I think Giles Shaw has simply gone through his officials to the security service and asked them, and they've said 'there's nothing in it, old boy'.[9]

Det. Chief Supt Cole interviewed Mr Dalyell at the House of Commons on 15 January 1985 but found the MP unwilling to disclose the sources of his information.

Mr Dalyell gave the detectives a long letter addressed to their Chief Constable, Robert Cozens. It read:

> I do wish to avoid a gratuitous quarrel and bad blood with the West Mercia police, when I do not think you are at fault. After Det. Supt Barry Maine phoned me on Christmas Eve, I did return to the sources of my information. In essence, what they repeat is this —
> 1. Towards the end of 1983, Sir Robert Armstrong, as

Secretary of the Cabinet, set up an inquiry into leaks, relating, inter alia, to GCHQ, Cheltenham, and *Belgrano* matters.

2. Various people were checked out. (You have my word for it that Clive Ponting is *not* the source of this information.)

3. In March 1984, there was a 'tremendous flap' in Downing Street.

4. In anticipation, however, of top-level ministerial meetings, involving the Prime Minister, Intelligence was told to do everything possible to identify the origin of the leaks of information about the *Belgrano*.

5. Under pressure to come up with information about the leaks, Intelligence decided to 'take a look' at the house of the aunt of Commander Robert Green.

Mr Dalyell concluded his letter by saying he could not reveal his sources of information. 'In general, who would ever trust a man who had revealed sources with information again? It is the dilemma of the journalist and the politician.

'In particular, however, in this case, I do not know the identity of Miss Murrell's killer. All I can do is to point you in the direction of those who, I believe, can help — and this I have done.'

Police and some Conservative MPs later joined forces in an attack on Mr Dalyell, accusing him of 'hindering the investigation' by wasting officers' time. Shrewsbury's Tory MP, Derek Conway, said he was concerned that Mr Dalyell's allegation was 'undermining confidence in the police. He has not produced one shred of evidence.'

Despite the ridicule, Mr Dalyell soldiered on. On 7 February 1985, he told readers of the *London Review of Books* why:

My first Parliamentary Question to the Home Office in November, before the inquest on Miss Murrell, [did not] elicit anything more than a routine reply. I therefore had to go quietly to friends to make inquiries.

In such situations I chose friends on the basis of their likely position to know, of their track record of accuracy in the past, and, above all, of their willingness to tell me bluntly if I am barking up the wrong tree.

The truth is that unless he has friends who are prepared to play the kind of role that 'Deep Throat' played in the unfolding Watergate saga, the politician will get nowhere. An MP without contacts would simply be wasting his time floundering around in the dark, and would be vulnerable to being made an ass of. In essence, what one deep throat told me was this . . .

Towards the end of December 1983, Sir Robert Armstrong, as Secretary of the Cabinet, set up an inquiry into leaks, relating, *inter alia*, to GCHQ Cheltenham and *Belgrano* matters.

Various people were checked out, either known or unbeknown to themselves. In March 1984 there was a 'tremendous flap' in Downing Street.

My attention was drawn, in particular, to what Mr Heseltine, the Defence Secretary, had said publicly to the Select Committee on Foreign Affairs, concerning his own activities in middle and late March and his contacts with Mrs Thatcher over how they should handle the *Belgrano* affair at that time . . .

On 22 March, the day incidentally on which Mr Ian Scott, a Shropshire farmer, was counting his trees with a view to felling in the very coppice in which Miss Murrell's body was to be found two days later, Mr Heseltine began his investigation into the documents which have come to be known as the Crown Jewels. (The Crown Jewels were a collection of papers prepared by Ministry of Defence civil servant Clive Ponting which detail all the known movements and signals relating to the *Belgrano*.)

On 29 March he [Mr Heseltine] received the Crown Jewels. What did the Secretary of State for Defence do then?

In his own words to the Select Committee, 'I immediately had an internal meeting and I had a meeting with the Prime Minister, and a further meeting on the Sunday, because I was going to Nato on the Monday, in order to decide what advice I would give the Prime Minister as to how we should deal with these questions.'

Among the readers of the *London Review of Books* [continued Mr Dalyell] there must be a goodly number of people who know jolly well how the uppermost echelons of Government work in this country: how often,

I ask them, in their experience, do they know of Defence
Secretaries scurrying off to see the Prime Minister, par-
ticularly *this* Prime Minister, about how to answer an
MP's questions?

How often do they call the inconvenient, short-notice
Sunday meeting? Not unless there is good cause!

A deep throat told me that in anticipation of all.this
ministerial and Prime Ministerial activity, Intelligence
was asked to do everything possible to identify the
origin of the leaks about the *Belgrano*.

Deep throat told me that, under pressure to come up
with information about the leaks, and remembering that
there was the related row about trade union rights at
GCHQ, Intelligence decided to 'take a look' at the house
of the aunt of Commander Robert Green.

Another deep throat added that the investigating
police should not be content with the bland assurances
given by Bernard Sheldon (the official spokesman for
MI5), Sir Robert Armstrong and Mr Peter Marychurch
(director of GCHQ), and some of their subordinates—
and indeed, the head of the Security Services, the Prime
Minister—on how much they had been told of the
Hilda Murrell case and when they were told of it.

I do appreciate that it is a bit of a tall order to suggest
that a local police force, even one as courteous, compet-
ent and professional as I found West Mercia to be, should
set about interviewing the Cabinet Secretary, let alone the
Prime Minister.

The truth of the matter is that a local police force
should not be in a position of being asked by an MP to
turn towards the most exalted figures in the land.

What there should be is an authority to which those
genuinely concerned about British Intelligence are able
to turn, and this should be a Select Committee of the
House of Commons—maybe composed of Privy Councillors.

Mr Dalyell's theory about a *Belgrano*-related break-in at
Hilda Murrell's home was reinforced by another unsolved
burglary, this time far from Shrewsbury.

Mr Dalyell made his startling allegation during a Consolid-
ated Fund Bill debate at 4 o'clock in the morning. Before

news of his claims were reported in the following day's
newspapers, the St Albans flat of Lt.-Commander Peter
Hurst was broken into. Lt.-Commander Hurst worked with
Rob Green at Northwood during the Falklands war. The
two are friends, sharing broadly similar views. Apart from
those who have retired from Northwood because of their
age, Lt.-Commander Hurst and Lt.-Commander Green are
the only senior men to have quit since the end of the
Falklands crisis.

Lt.-Commander Hurst's flat was the only one in the block
to be burgled, although it is on neither the top or ground
floors. His papers were searched but the only thing stolen
was a small quantity of alcohol. An expensive stereo
system, video and television were untouched. Commander
Hurst, who now works for British Aerospace, believes his
telephone has been tapped and that he is under surveillance
because of his Falklands' work.[10]

In March 1985 I sought to test Mr Dalyell's claim by seek-
ing further information from two official Intelligence chiefs,
Mr Marychurch and Sir Robert Armstrong. I wrote to Mr
Marychurch on 6 March:

Dear Mr Marychurch,

I am writing to ask if you can help me with my research
for material which might be included in a book about
the murder of Miss Hilda Murrell.

You have probably heard of Miss Murrell's murder; she
died nearly a year ago and the subsequent police hunt
for her killer has received nationwide publicity, particularly since Tam Dalyell MP raised the subject in the
House of Commons on 19 December 1984.

What I want to know is:

(a) When did you first learn of Miss Murrell's murder?
(b) Who told you?

I would be very pleased to meet you for a face-to-face
interview if you think that would be preferable to reply-
ing by letter.

I would also like to know when, if at all, you first learned
of a burglary at the St Albans flat of Peter Hurst, a
former naval intelligence officer. Again, if you can
remember who told you about it I would be most
interested to know.

I appreciate that you probably do not receive many
letters like this one asking for information about
murders and other assorted mysteries, but I do assure you
that mine is a perfectly straightforward and genuine
attempt to discover if the claims made in the House of
Commons by Mr Dalyell can be substantiated.
I look forward to hearing from you.
Yours sincerely,
Graham Smith

Mr Marychurch did not reply. A similar letter to Sir
Robert Armstrong brought this response from his Private
Secretary, Mr R.P. Hatfield:

In answer to your inquiry, Sir Robert Armstrong has
asked me to say that he has no official knowledge
relating to the case of Miss Murrell although he has of
course seen the publicity given to the case following Mr
Dalyell's intervention in the House of Commons last
December.[11]

Police have admitted they have sought information from
and about many of Miss Murrell's friends. Anyone who
might be connected with the peace or environmen movements who was known to have been in contact with Miss
Murrell was investigated. 'Our lines of inquiry have embraced all the organisations to which Miss Murrell belonged or
expressed an interest in and her involvement in conservation matters concerning nuclear waste,' said police. Mr
Dalyell is convinced that his 'deep throats' are supplying
him with accurate information, and that Miss Murrell's
murder was an accidental by-product of a *Belgrano*-related
search of her home by British Intelligence. Anyone who
knows Mr Dalyell will know that he is not given to making
wild claims unless he believes sincerely that they are true.
If the information he has been given *is* accurate, it begs a
vital question: what is it about the sinking of the *Belgrano*
which is so secret that British Intelligence could be led to
kill Hilda Murrell?

A Politician's Tale

Tam Dalyell MP is not the only politician to have spoken in
the House of Commons about the murder of Hilda Murrell.
Any idea that the inquiry into her death had become a one-
man Parliamentary campaign would be quite wrong.

The House of Commons was an unusually busy place for
a 4 am sitting on 19 December 1984. A Labour Front Bench
Spokesman, Clive Soley MP, was on hand to add his contrib-
ution. So too was Rob Green's own constituency MP, the
Liberal Paddy Ashdown. Home Office Minister Giles Shaw
was there to field their questions. Several other MPs, expect-
ing an early morning sensation, had also taken their seats.
Mr Ashdown followed Mr Dalyell into the Hilda Murrell
controversy. He told the Commons that he had checked Mr
Dalyell's allegations with Rob Green *before* they were
raised in Parliament:

> Commander Bob Green is a member of the Liberal
> association in my constituency. One does not neces-
> sarily have to agree with the conclusions that the hon.
> Member [Mr Dalyell] has reached to recognise fully the
> serious nature of the questions he has rightly put and
> which need to be answered.
>
> First let me deal with some of the facts. I have not
> carried out detailed research into the facts put forward
> by the hon. Member. However, I have the highest respect
> for Commander Bob Green. I asked the hon. Member if
> I could ring Commander Green and read his speech to
> him. The hon. Member allowed me to do so. Therefore I
> rang Commander Green and read to him the speech of
> the hon. Member.
>
> I have his authority to say that he confirms and cor-
> roborates all that the hon. Member has said. The details
> and facts are precisely as Commander Green sees them.
> Where the hon. Member has referred to Commander
> Green, Commander Green assures me that he agrees with
> the hon. Member's references.
>
> It is also fair and proper to make the point that Com-
> mander Green has in no way collaborated with the hon.

59

Member for Linlithgow [Mr Dalyell] in drawing up his
speech. Commander Green has had no contact whatsoever with the hon. Member.[1]

Mr Ashdown then went on to distance himself from the
conclusions drawn by Mr Dalyell, but it is interesting to note
that in so far as the *facts* are concerned, there was no
dispute. Mr Dalyell's information, as we have seen, came
from anonymous 'Deep Throats'. They had, at least, got
their facts correct. Mr Ashdown said he did not necessarily
agree with the implications behind some of Mr Dalyell's
questions, but nevertheless called for a full inquiry.

'I believe there is only one way forward,' he said, 'a full
inquiry in front of a High Court judge. I hope that other
hon. Members will support that kind of inquiry. We do not
call at this stage for such an inquiry. We merely say that if
the Minister is unable or unwilling to answer questions of
fact in detail, that is the only proper way forward.'[2]

Unfortunately, although Giles Shaw promised he would
answer all the questions in a 'proper and comprehensive'
way, he did in the end issue only a brief, dismissive statement saying that Mr Dalyell's allegations were 'without
foundation'. Paddy Ashdown conceded that Hilda Murrell's
murder was unlikely to have been authorised by the security services. 'If what [Mr Dalyell] says is true,' added Mr
Ashdown, 'there must have been a significant breakdown in
the way that our Intelligence Services are controlled . . .
either a politician at a very high level was involved in taking
a decision to allow such action to go ahead, or there must
have been a very serious breakdown in the democratic and
political accountability and control of our Intelligence
Services.'[3]

Paddy Ashdown himself is a former member of the Special
Boat Service and included his expertise in winding up his
speech. 'There are many people, including me, who, because
of friends and contacts, have reason to worry that the traditional and appropriate control of this country's Intelligence
Service has become much looser than appropriate and much
less regulated than is necessary within a democracy.'[4]

Labour's Front Bench Spokesman on Home Affairs, Clive
Soley, then contributed to the debate. He said the story told
by Mr Dalyell 'would tax the ingenuity of a novelist' but

warned against dismissing the allegations. 'We should
remember that truth can be stranger than fiction,' he went
on.

Mr Soley paid tribute to Mr Dalyell's campaign to uncover
facts about the sinking of the *Belgrano*, and warned that
there were more facts to come about the murder of Hilda
Murrell.

'Not only is [Tam Dalyell's] research accurate,' said Mr
Soley, 'but so are the sources of his information. I know
those to be extremely good sources of information. The
Minister and many others must be deeply disturbed by the
quality of the information that is always available to my hon.
Friend. He uses that information to deploy his case well.'

Mr Soley ended his speech by calling for reform in the
accountability of the security services and backed Mr
Dalyell's call for more information about Hilda Murrell.
'My hon. Friend,' concluded Mr Soley, 'by the way in which
he has brought the matter out, has done a service not only
to the House but to the nation as well.'[5]

It then befell Mr Shaw to answer Mr Dalyell's allegations.
He played a dead bat to most of the questions, and was unusually courteous about Mr Dalyell, who has in the past
been an object for Tory ridicule and contempt.

'It may be considered odd,' said Mr Shaw, 'if there were
a British security element involved in the investigation, or
occasioning the crime for which the investigation has been
set up, that it should continue without those involved being
able to ensure that the police and the security services are
sharing common knowledge.'

Here, for the first time, was a Home Office Minister
admitting before Parliament that if the security services
were involved in the murder of Hilda Murrell, they would
find it easy to remain one step ahead of any subsequent
police attempt to catch them.[6]

Mr Shaw then read from a brief which followed closely
the version of events as described by the police. Concluding,
he promised that the questions asked by Mr Dalyell, supported by Mr Ashdown and Mr Soley, 'deserve and will
obtain a proper and considered response.'

The response, when it came, may have been 'considered'
but it did not stop the questions. Three months after the
Commons' debate, on 15 March 1985, Labour's Front

Bench Foreign Affairs Spokesman, George Foulkes MP, called on the Prime Minister to order an inquiry into what he called 'this tangled web of intrigue'.

He said: 'The whole thing is getting sinister. I am getting increasingly suspicious that there is more to this than meets the eye. Like the whole *Belgrano* incident, I suspect that more is going to filter out.'[7]

The questions are still being asked. Whether they will *ever* be answered, however, is another matter.

A Chief Constable's Tale

WEST MERCIA POLICE ANSWER THEIR CRITICS

Not surprisingly, the police have reacted angrily to criticisms of their methods and their failure to catch Hilda Murrell's murderer. A spokesman said: 'We've had every amateur detective in the country putting forward hair-brained schemes and theories about the killing. It's got to the stage now that it is seriously hindering our inquiries because officers are having to waste time following up leads which don't exist.'

The West Mercia Constabulary issued an 11-page statement[1] which they hoped would end speculation about the murder. It said:

> In view of the speculation over certain areas of this inquiry and in order to dispel confusion, the following statement is made:—

> *Involvement of British Intelligence officers*
> Mr Tam Dalyell, MP for Linlithgow, has apparently alleged in the House of Commons on 19 December 1984 that he had been informed that men of the British Intelligence service were searching Miss Murrell's house when she disturbed them. They had then injured her and panicked.
>
> Police inquiries to date reveal no evidence to suggest the involvement of British Intelligence officers in this murder, nor has there been any approach whatsoever to the police from any agency to engage in a 'cover up' of the facts. Arrangements have been made for senior detectives to interview Mr Dalyell on 15 January 1985 concerning his allegations. Any information he has concerning this inquiry will be analysed and acted upon accordingly.

> *Suspended officers*
> It has been previously reported in the press that three Crime Squad officers working on the Murrell case have been suspended from duty. It has been further quoted in the press that Mr Dalyell questions whether the officers had been given the impression that this case was one which should not come to an outcome. This is very far

63

from true—senior officers on the murder inquiry carrying out their supervisory duties became aware of discrepancies in these officers' duties and reported it to the DCC (Deputy Chief Constable) who implemented disciplinary procedures and caused them to be suspended. That disciplinary inquiry continues.

Sizewell Inquiry

In the early stages of this inquiry, certain suggestions were raised that Miss Murrell may have been killed because of her views against the use of nuclear power. Our lines of inquiry have embraced all the organisations to which Miss Murrell belonged or expressed an interest in and her involvement in conservation matters concerning nuclear waste.

After a full assessment of the inquiry into this aspect it is not being further pursued at this time.

Two specific points could be made here:—

Firstly, two copies of Miss Murrell's report on the Sizewell project were openly available on the table of one of the rooms which the intruder searched. This report was subsequently read to the Sizewell inquiry by Miss Murrell's nephew, Lt.-Commander Robert Denton Green (retired).

Secondly, the report prepared by Miss Murrell was independently assessed and the composite opinion was that whilst it was well written it contained no new or startling revelations.

Special Branch

It should be understood that specialist officers are often called upon to perform non-specialist roles when the man-power demands are great. This has been the situation in this case and Special Branch officers have been used on the routine murder inquiry work.

In addition to that role, Special Branch officers were used to inquire into the Sizewell B aspect. They were used because it was felt that their experience particularly fitted them to deal with this inquiry.

Hypnotist

A number of potential witnesses have undergone a process of hypnosis by two qualified practitioners under strictly controlled conditions closely adhering to rules laid down

by the Metropolitan Police in an attempt to gain information which they were unable to recall through normal
memory processes.

Although this is an uncommon step, it is not unique
in murder inquiries and was only taken after due consideration. It achieved a certain measure of success in that
these witnesses did recall further details which have been
incorporated into the police search for the murderer.
Details of the use of an hypnotist in this case were released to the press in May 1984.

FBI

Full details of the involvement of the FBI were released
to the media in September 1984. It has been suggested
that the FBI was called in to investigate the murder of
Miss Murrell — this is not so.

The West Mercia police have maintained an open-
minded approach to this inquiry and have not felt reluctant
to seek or receive help from any quarter. Accordingly, data
concerning the case, collected over a period of months,
was forwarded to the FBI behavioural science research
department. This data was analysed to prepare a criminal
personality profile of the offender. Their reply was closely
aligned to the views formed by the senior local investigating
officer. Extracts of this profile were circulated on TV and
in the press describing this man as a white male in his 30s, a
loner who had a liking for drink, probably an unskilled man
living or working locally with an uncertain temper. The
public responded with many suggestions, some made anon-
ymously on a tape phone specially fitted at Shrewsbury HQ.
All suggestions were evaluated and investigated.

Sequence of events leading to finding the body
Miss Murrell's Renault car was seen in the ditch at
Hunkington on 21 March 1984 by a local farmer who
notified an off-duty police officer at 5.20 pm. Officers
went to the scene within an hour but there were no
apparent suspicious circumstances. There was only
superficial damage to the car and no apparent danger or
obstruction to any member of the public. The officers,
therefore, made a preliminary search of the immediate
area, but took no further action at that stage. They
checked the registration of the vehicle with the Police

E

National Computer and were given the correct name and address of the keeper.

To put the matter into perspective, research carried out for the Divisional Police Commander shows that in the first quarter of 1984, over 250 vehicles were abandoned in this area during 1984 for various reasons, e.g. drivers visiting beauty spots, simple mechanical break-downs, minor accidents, etc, etc. The majority of these vehicles are recovered by their owners within 48 hours.

The officer had intended to re-check the vehicle the following day but due to operational committments was unable to do so. On Friday, 23 March 1984, the farmer contacted the police informing them that the vehicle was still in situ.

Attempts to telephone the registered keeper had proved unsuccessful and therefore an officer made a personal visit to the house in Sutton Road at 7 pm.

On arrival the officer found a door insecure and a light was on within the premises. However, signs apparent to the police officer at that time suggested that the premises were normally occupied and that the owner was absent for only a short period. For this reason the officer resumed patrol with a request that further attempts be made to contact the occupier.

Early on the morning of Saturday, 24 March 1984, another police officer visited the house and found the door still insecure, locked it, making further inquiries with neighbours and relatives.

Concern over Miss Murrell's absence increased and the police efforts to trace her were accordingly intensified. As a result, at approximately 10.20 am, another police officer, in company with the local gamekeeper's wife and her dogs, found the body of Miss Murrell in a coppice some 500 yards across a corn field from where her car was abandoned.

Search for red Escort car
There are seven sightings of a red car, either near the deceased' house, or relatively near to the area where the body was found, within several days of the murder. The three most significant are:— a sighting of a red saloon car parked on the road near the deceased's house at

about 10.15 on 21 March 1984; a red Escort was noted travelling around the Hunkington Lane area three times on Friday, 23 March 1984; a local farmer recollects seeing a red Escort-type vehicle driving past the farm twice on Sunday, 25 March 1984.

Although there is no direct evidence linking a red Escort vehicle to Miss Murrell's death, the police obviously were keen to trace the drivers of these vehicles. Road checks were set up at the Hunkington area and Sutton Road area. Press appeals made, computer searches carried out and many owners of such vehicles interviewed, but we have not traced the drivers of the cars concerned.

The matter was further complicated when police received information that a red Escort was seen to drive away from the gateway near the murder scene on 21 March 1984. This was investigated and it was discovered that this information was utterly false and deliberately passed to the police to mislead them.

Sexual assault

At the very early stages of the inquiry there was no immediate evidence to suggest that Miss Murrell had been sexually assaulted in any way and this was referred to by Det. Chief Supt Cole at a press conference on 26 March 1984.

As the inquiry progressed, however, evidence was found to show that she had, in fact, been subjected to some form of sexual activity. This evidence indicates that what in legal terms could be construed as a sexual assault occurred, but the term 'sexual activity' was used to avoid further distress to relatives.

Some confusion, however, has occurred over two police press releases. In answer to a direct question, had she been raped, the police replied No. But we did say later that the deceased had been subjected to some form of sexual activity. Both these statements are true and are not contradictory; however, certain newspapers have misconstrued them as such. It is not intended that any further details on this particular aspect will be released for two reasons:—

(a) To ensure that no further distress is caused to Miss

Murrell's family and friends and
(b) Operational reasons concerning future interviews.

Ransacking of Ravenscroft

On 9 November 1984 an article appeared in the *New Statesman* which claimed that, 'The first information released by the police, to the press, was that Miss Murrell's house had been ransacked.' The article went on to say that this 'Police claim' turned out to be untrue.

This is in fact a total misquote of police statements. It was initially released by police, and is still maintained, that the house had been thoroughly searched by the intruder. The expression 'ransacked', therefore, can only be attributed to journalist interpretation.

The house was searched thoroughly and systematically, but this showed all the hallmarks of an experienced burglar and was not consistent with an intruder whose intention was to conceal the very fact that he had entered and searched the premises.

Moving of the body

As previously stated, the body of Hilda Murrell was found on the morning of Saturday, 24 March 1984 in a copse known locally as Hunkington Moat.

The police have been aware from the outset that one witness, a local farmer in the Upton Magna area, has stated that he was in the Moat Wood at approximately 3.30 pm on 22 March 1984, and that he did not see Miss Murrell's body.

This has been carefully considered and researched. He may be mistaken. The body was in a slight hollow and dressed in clothing which matched the undergrowth.

It is more likely that the body was not moved after coming to rest in the copse as the Home Office pathologist stated at the inquest--that death was likely to have occurred within five to ten hours of the stabbing attack on her and that hyperstatis was consistent with the position in which the body was found.

Telephone

Originally the matter of telephone disconnection was not released to the press owing to an operational need to retain certain details. However, this matter has now been

made public, via the *New Statesman* article. It is therefore
incumbent upon us to clarify several points.

The telephone at Ravenscroft had been rendered partly
inoperative; however, the manner in which this was
achieved cannot be described as sophisticated and this term
has not been used to the press by the police. The phone
could be used to ring out, but its own bell would not sound.
A person making a call to Ravenscroft would hear a ringing
out tone despite the fact that the bell was inoperative

The telephone at Llanymynech malfunctioned due to a
capacitor fault caused by storm damage and is in no way
consistent with human interference to the premises. Both
appliances have been independently assessed by a British
Telecom engineer.

Further details cannot be expanded upon for the afore-
mentioned reasons.

Second post mortem and disposal of the body
The reason for the second post mortem on Miss Murrell's
body has been questioned. The answer is straightforward:—
The body began to deteriorate and, as a result, the
Director of Public Prosecutions directed that a second
independent autopsy be carried out to protect the interests
of anyone subsequently arrested for Miss Murrell's murder.
It has also been said that the relatives were required to
move the body with undue haste. As previously stated, the
body was deteriorating rapidly. After the decision had
been made that the body could not be left indefinitely
because of this factor, then the arrangements concerning
disposal are a matter for the hospital authorities and the
undertakers and not for the police.

Facilities for storing the body for an excessive period
are not available in the Shropshire area and, in view of
the fact that a second autopsy had already been carried
out, it was not felt necessary to ask the coroner to allow
for alternative arrangements to be made elsewhere.

Police view of the offence
It is the view of senior detectives investigating this case
that the murder is the result of a burglary which went
tragically wrong. In coming to this conclusion it is necessary to make assumptions and deductions. Whilst it is
accepted that these may not necessarily be one hundred

per cent accurate, they are nevertheless based on considerable experience and a thorough review of the facts.
Some of the facts are:—
Firstly, the house appears to have been thoroughly
searched but documents have not been disturbed.

Various receptacles which might have contained money
have been opened.

We have evidence to show that Miss Murrell withdrew
£50 from her bank that Wednesday morning. We know
that £3.10 of that money was subsequently spent at a
local shop. The remainder is missing, believed stolen by
the intruder and handbags in the house had been searched.
This, together with the other points mentioned previously,
does tend to refute suggestions that burglary was not the
motive.

There is evidence in the house to suggest a struggle
after Miss Murrell confronted the intruder—an incident
consistent with her known strong-minded character.
Evidence suggests that the intruder had panicked after the
confrontation.

Miss Murrell had been subjected to some form of sexual activity, an element known to sometimes occur during
the emotionally heightened experience of house burglary
where the burglar confronts a female occupant

The public are reminded that the police still have a full
Incident Room and inquiry teams working on this case.
It is very much a live inquiry and is being pursued with
vigour. Any information, however seemingly insignificant,
will be welcomed and carefully reviewed.

This long statement was issued by police in January 1985;
I have referred to parts of it earlier in this book. The statement was followed by another press release, dated 28 January 1985:

Response to letter from Mr Tam Dalyell
The Chief Constable of West Mercia, Mr Robert Cozens,
today issued the following statement:

During his recent interview at the House of Commons,
Mr Tam Dalyell gave my officers a letter addressed to me
concerning the death of Miss Hilda Murrell.

I have also received a full report from the officers who

conducted the interview. Having studied that report, I
have now replied to Mr Dalyell and a copy of my letter
is attached.

The letter thanked Mr Dalyell for the interview and continued:

> I hope you will understand if I limit my comments to my
> role in the investigation of the death of Miss Murrell and
> leave you to pursue the political issues elsewhere. I
> appreciate that you feel the two aspects are connected
> but the nub of this matter is the discovery of evidence to
> support your view and I will confine myself to this
> central point.
>
> A careful assessment of the information, written and
> oral, that you provided at your interview has now been
> completed but has produced no evidence to lend sub-
> stance to your claim that there is a link between the
> death of Miss Murrell and 'British Intelligence'. The writ-
> ten material you gave my officers consists mainly of a
> collection of speculative articles, letters or remarks from
> various sources but none of it provides any evidence to
> support what can best be described as rumours. Regret-
> tably this also applies to the answers you gave to my
> officers at your interview.
>
> I was therefore puzzled to read in *The Times* your state-
> ment made immediately after the interview with my
> officers that it is 'a matter of fact that Intelligence
> intruders went into the house of Hilda Murrell on March
> 21'.
>
> Whilst I respect your reluctance to identify the source
> of your information in this case, the investigation of a
> death occurring in these circumstances is an extremely
> serious matter and if you think your informant has
> evidence which could assist us then you have a public
> duty to encourage the person to come forward. I give you
> my assurance that any evidence that is forthcoming will
> be very thoroughly investigated.

> Yours sincerely,
> Robert Cozens
> Chief Constable

At the time of writing (March 1985), the detectives who were suspended are still off-duty. 'Inquiries into their behaviour are continuing and they remain suspended,' said a police spokesman.[2] The police are making no moves to investigate the private detectives who are known to have been spying on Sizewell B objectors. 'There was nothing in *The Observer* report of 27 January 1984 to link these private detectives directly with Miss Murrell,' said the spokesman. 'Nothing which has been said, none of the speculation or wild theories, have brought any positive new lines of inquiry.'

The only new development has been Mr Cozens's decision to call in senior officers from the Northumbria constabulary to review his own detectives' handling of the Hilda Murrell case. Northumbria's assistant Chief Constable, Peter Smith, aided by two of his colleagues, is examining the way the West Mercia police conducted their investigation and hopes to suggest new lines of inquiry.

'I am here at the invitation of the West Mercia police,' said Mr Smith, 'and I hope I can help. It is not at all unusual for officers from an outside force to be called in when an inquiry has been going on for a long time and does not imply any criticism of the way West Mercia has handled the case.'[3]

Mr Cozens, meanwhile, is quitting the police force. He is taking a civilian job as head of police research services at the Home Office.

A Nephew's Tale

ROB GREEN RAISES MORE QUESTIONS

Hilda Murrell lived alone and was a shy, retiring person who chose her friends carefully. The person she was closest to was her nephew, Rob Green, who has speculated that his aunt was murdered because of her objections to the Sizewell B project. He now works as a thatcher in Dorset, but is continuing to probe his aunt's killing.

'Hilda had a passionate love for the British countryside and wildlife and was very expert at it,' said Rob Green.

> She devoted the last years of her life to this. She saw pollution of the environment as being a new and very dangerous problem and thought the nuclear industry were producing the worst of all pollutants.
>
> She would write letters to either *The Times* or *The Guardian*, which were the two newspapers she was reading at that time. She also wrote to the Prime Minister and to other ministers, and as she began to write more directly and in some detail she actually succeeded in getting her letters through to Ministers who had to deal with them.
>
> When she went to the CND demo in London in 1983 she sent me a copy of her Sizewell papers and asked me to present them at the inquiry if anything should happen to her. I suppose *that*, for the first time, did raise in our minds the possibility that she was taking seriously the possibility that someone might try to stop her giving evidence.[1]

Commander Green believes it is possible that the intruder at his aunt's home did not run away when her car drew up on the gravel outside because he knew she had a luncheon appointment. 'I speculate that it is because he hadn't finished what he was going to do, or that he felt he might be able to conceal himself, knowing she was still going to lunch,' he said.

He then described how Miss Murrell would have reacted on confronting an intruder at her home:

> She would have said, 'You can take anything you want

of my valuables' and if they had shown the slightest
sign of not wanting to then she would have very quickly
jumped to the conclusion that it was her papers they were
after, and it would have been her anti-nuclear papers.

She once said that if she was ever burgled, she would
not fight over her possessions, but she would fight over
her papers. I believe that was entirely characteristic, and
that she would be absolutely fearless. She would have
fought like a cat.

I just find it quite incredible that a simple burglar,
going for cash, would take this enormous risk of
abducting her. I just speculate that he couldn't risk just
clearing off, leaving her to tell the world.

No doubt he didn't have the authority anyway to kill
her and so was left with the dilemma of how to keep
control of her while wanting to get higher authority or
advice on what to do next.[2]

In Commander Green's view, the burglar's motive explains
the strange route he took having abducted Miss Murrel in her
own car. Instead of turning right out of her drive into the
country, he turned left into the centre of Shrewsbury. He
actually drove past the police station, with Miss Murrell
slumped in the passenger seat.

'I am drawn to believe that he wanted to go along that
route for some other reason that was over-riding,' said Rob
Green. 'Perhaps he was going to a rendezvous with an accomplice, and that accomplice was somewhere along that route.'

Rob Green also believes his aunt did not die in the copse
where her body was found three days later, but was instead
dumped behind the hedge off the side of the road. Her killer
would otherwise have had to carry her 500 yards to the spot
where her body was discovered.

I think the distance is so great, that the chances of him
carrying her across there without being seen are very
small. You have to bear in mind the fact that it was
lunchtime on a clear, sunny day and that this is a well-
known beauty spot where it is not unusual to see casual
visitors. Perhaps the assailant did not know whether she
was dead or not when he left her and then tried to
confuse the trail in some way, because the car was still

there, waiting to be reported and followed up. That was a very risky situation.[3]

Commander Green believes the killer might have returned to Miss Murrell's house after the abduction.

I've always wondered why it was that the intruder chose that day to break into the house. I understand that her luncheon date was the only social engagement in her diary for that week, and therefore I am led to believe that in some way maybe her telephone was tapped.

Hilda was suspicious that her telephone was tapped and was therefore very discreet when talking over the phone, particularly about her Sizewell paper.[4]

Commander Green believes that of all the theories about Hilda Murrell's murder, the possibility that she was killed 'by some crank' connected with the nuclear power industry is the most likely. He is continuing his own investigation into his aunt's mysterious death.

End of the Tale?

If this were an ordinary detective novel then this would be the last chapter, in which I dismissed all the red-herrings and stunningly revealed that Hilda Murrell was in fact murdered by her butler.

Unfortunately, Miss Murrell did not have a butler and I don't know who killed her. But I hope this book does have one advantage over an ordinary detective novel: it is a work of fact, not fiction. Perhaps we can learn something from a review of all the evidence presented so far.

It is, on the face of it, very strange that in spite of all the police reassurances about Miss Murrell's death, speculation has persisted that she was killed by someone even more sinister than an ordinary burglar.

It has to be said that some of the speculation, no doubt quite unfair, is the result of Det. Chief Supt Cole's personal involvement in the murder hunt. Just as the police naturally suspect people who have had previous involvement with crime, so too do some radicals suspect officials who have a known track record of associating closely with the security services.

Det. Chief Supt Cole is a vastly experienced detective. He has brought many murderers to justice and has an enviable success record.

Det. Chief Supt Cole is also the policeman who arrested and brought to justice the GCHQ spy, Geoffrey Prime. Mr Prime is now in prison for selling secrets to the Russians. His treachery caused much embarrassment to the Foreign Office and annoyance to the United States. Det. Chief Supt Cole will no doubt have learned much about the shadowy world of the Special Branch and MI5 during his investigation into the Prime spying case and will have developed a good working relationship with the security services. There is no suggestion whatever that Det. Chief Supt Cole's relationship with MI5 in any way undermined his determination to catch Hilda Murrell's killer. But would he be compromised if he had to undertake an investigation of MI5? Even if he were not, would it not lower public confidence in the police and security services?

I will say only that this suggestion is every bit as unfair as the police automatically suspecting people of a crime just because they have previous convictions. The police investigation into Miss Murrell's murder, however, does beg many questions about their handling of the case. I appreciate that we are now moving towards an area of unsubstantiated speculation, but what is wrong with that? The police also can only speculate, and have done so right from day one of the inquiry. Theories *must* be devised to fit the facts because facts cannot be twisted to fit theories. Even so, there can still be an infinite number of theories.

The *facts* I will now discuss are the same as those available to the police. The conclusions I reach are very different, however, and lead me to conclude that either the police *are* party to a cover-up, or they are to a degree incompetent because they have not seriously investigated *all* the possibilities. The police have been less than even-handed in their treatment of known facts.

For example, the police spent much time and energy asking the public for information about a red Escort car which was seen in the vicinity of Miss Murrell's home on the day of the murder and later in the area where her body was found. Has it not occurred to the police that if this red car is in *any* way connected with the murder, then it is likely there will have been at least *two* people involved in the killing? The person who abducted Miss Murrell did so in her Renault. Who was driving the Escort? The police say, quite properly, that they have no firm evidence to link the car directly with the murder. Why not apply the same standards of inquiry to the *fact* that objectors to the Sizewell B hearing were being spied on by private detectives? Or to the *fact* that naval intelligence staff who resigned after the Falklands war were being investigated as potential sources of leaks about the *Belgrano*?

Why will the police not discuss the death of a witness, during questioning, within a week of Miss Murrell's murder?

Why not release the full pathologists' reports?

More than a year after the killing, there can be few facts which need to remain secret for 'operational' reasons.

If it is within the gift of the West Mercia police categorically to refute either the Sizewell or *Belgrano* theories why have they not done so?

Is it not time to identify the three suspended detectives and so quash the rumour that they were playing golf because they knew the murderer was not meant to be caught?

The police have insisted from the start that the manner by which Miss Murrell's telephone was disabled was 'not sophisticated'. Sophisticated by whose standards? We are still left with the police failing to take seriously the claims that the telephone had been tampered with by someone who clearly knows more about these things than do most of us.

Why have the police been happy to assume that Miss Murrell's Llanymynech telephone was put out of action by lightning, when no one can remember any lightning in February or March?

In January 1985 the Llanymynech 'shack' was severely damaged in an arson attack. Such arson attacks are not uncommon on second homes in Wales. But, given the absence of any other leads, should the police not have looked more closely at this incident?

The police have insisted throughout that Miss Murrell was killed where she was found, even though the pathologist, Dr Acland, has agreed it is possible that she was either dragged to the copse or carried there by *two* people who carefully laid the body in such a position that no one would know.

The two boys who stole Miss Murrell's tax disc on the day she was abducted say there were papers in the back of her car. The police found no papers. So why have they not followed up more seriously the apparent theft of these papers?

Why did the burglar pick Wednesday, 21 March to go into Miss Murrell's home? We know there is a very strong possibility that her telephone was tapped. Could it be that the burglar *expected* her to be out that day, the *only* day on which she had made plans over the telephone to be away from home? Why have the police not attached greater weight to this possibility?

Most murders are solved within a few days. Is it not reasonable to ask, more than a year after the killing, why the police have not paid greater attention to the theories advanced by Miss Murrell's friends and relatives? Could it be that the police regard anti-nuclear protestors as half-witted cranks who should not be taken seriously? Or is there

another, even more sinister reason why the police have failed
to follow up these ideas?

I want now to explore some of these theories in greater
detail. They remain unsubstantiated speculation, but are no
less valid than the official view that the murderer was a
chance burglar seeking cash.

We know that Miss Murrell returned home unexpectedly
and, according to police, disturbed an intruder. It seems to
me more likely that she did not know the intruder was in
the house until he attacked her. Why else would the
struggle have taken place upstairs? Would Miss Murrell not
have noticed that her belongings had been disturbed on
entering her home? Yet Det. Chief Supt Cole told the
inquest that Miss Murrell had gone upstairs to get changed.

One possible explanation is that Miss Murrell's house was
not searched until *after* she had been abducted. This would
cover the otherwise baffling *fact* that her gardener and
neighbour noticed immediately the signs of a burglary as
soon as they went inside on the Saturday morning.

If we accept, for the moment, that the house was searched only *after* the abduction, we are still left with the
problem of a motive. But so too are the police. It must be
said that any post-abduction burglary could have been
carried out by a common thief. But this is highly unlikely.
More probable, if we follow this line of thinking, is that the
house was searched for information and that evidence was
then left to suggest either a sex or cash motive.

Now for the abduction itself. Notwithstanding the fact
that it is highly unusual for a common burglar to kidnap
his victim, no one disputes that the abduction was particularly strange. Why did the burglar not take Miss Murrell
straight into the countryside? The route he actually
followed took him straight past the police station in the
centre of town. It is possible, of course, that he did not know
where he was going. But the police believe they are looking
for a local man who knew the area. The police cannot have
it both ways. If the man *did* know where he was going, the
route is highly significant—*straight past the police station*.
Was the car being driven erratically *deliberately* to attract
attention, to signal something wrong? Again, the possibility
of an accomplice looms large.

So where and how did Miss Murrell die? There is no

evidence to suggest she was stabbed in either the house or in her car. Could it be possible that an unconscious Miss Murrell was transferred from her Renault to another car, perhaps a red Escort, on the Wednesday but that she was not killed and her body not dumped until the Thursday evening?

Local people remember seeing lights moving in the copse at that time. Could they have been torches? Anyone in the copse after dark would certainly not have been tourists enjoying the beauty-spot!

The conclusion we must reach is that the twin conspiracy theories of a Sizewell or *Belgrano* connection, in purely practical terms, are both perfectly possible. Whether they are likely or not is another matter. I do not believe the West Mercia Constabulary are, as a police force, capable of organising such a conspiracy. There is no way you could have 120 detectives involved in a cover-up. Any conspiracy on the part of the police would have to be limited to fewer than six (or less) senior officers who might send their detectives on fools' errands. It seems quite incredible that there would have been information at Miss Murrell's home which was actually worth breaking in for. *We* know she had no papers connected with the *Belgrano*. But the security services did not know. So the theory stands.

Miss Murrell is not known to have had any particularly original views about the disposal of radioactive waste. But given the rather twisted private detectives who are known to have been spying on the Sizewell objectors, we cannot dismiss the possibility that Miss Murrell was among those being spied on, or the subsequent theory that the burglar was after nuclear information.

Both Rob Green and Gerard Morgan-Grenville incline towards the theory that Miss Murrell's death was connected with the nuclear industry.

'The nuclear lobby—the Atomic Energy Authority, the Central Electricity Generating Board and British Nuclear Fuels Ltd—they are known to be very worried about damaging information which shows them in a bad light,' said Mr Morgan-Grenville. 'In other countries, the nuclear authorities routinely instigate inquiries to try to find the sources of leaks of information. I don't see any reason why the same should not be true in this country.' Rob Green and Mr Morgan-Grenville believe that Tam Dalyell might have been 'set up' either by someone who wanted to damage his *Belgrano* campaign or to deflect suspicion from the nuclear industry.

Against this, we must take into account the fact that Victor Norris actually began his snooping on Sizewell objectors more than a year before Miss Murrell was killed. And the last person to see Miss Murrell alive, her lifelong friend Mrs Frances O'Connor, says that Miss Murrell was *not* concerned or worried that anyone might be after her.

Only Tam Dalyell knows the identity of his 'deep throats' and therefore only Mr Dalyell can vouch for their credibility. But by doing so he puts his own credibility on the line and that is something he would not do unless he was convinced he was right.

When I raised the question with Mr Dalyell he replied:

Am I being set-up in getting this information?

I don't think so. From one of the sources, seemingly unlikely information on the *Belgrano* has turned out to be wholly accurate.

Am I lying? I have no great faith in lie-detectors, but I am quite willing to submit to a polygraph test, if the police think it useful.

Perhaps Sir Robert Armstrong, Mr Marychurch and Mrs Thatcher, who seem to have great faith in polygraphs for other people would care to submit themselves to the lie-detector if necessary?

As a result, I must say that my personal preference is for the *Belgrano* theory, but as a coward I have to confess that I would like to hedge my bets if I could!

I do not rule out the possibility of a Sizewell-related motive and indeed to be fair to the proponents of this theory, I should for the record say that Tam Dalyell himself is one of the strongest advocates for the nuclear power industry.

Being really cowardly, however, I would remind you of what I said at the outset of Chapter 4: we cannot rule out the possibility that the police might be right and that the killer *was* just a chance burglar seeking cash and, or, sex.

The only honest answer to the question: Who killed Hilda Murrell? is that I do not know. The purpose in writing this book, however, is to make sure that the question is not forgotten.

A Spook's Tale

Although a full account of the work of the security services
is far beyond the scope of this book, the issues raised by
the widespread public concern over Hilda Murrell's death
merit a few words to outline some of the essential points
which have been publicly known for several years.

The security services essentially consist of three elements,
MI5, MI6 and the Special Branch. MI6 is supposedly concerned with espionage (spying on other countries), MI5 with
counter-espionage (spying on other countries' spies) and the
Special Branch is recruited from the ordinary police force —
although it works closely with MI5. The Special Branch is
particularly active in spying on trade unions, especially
when they are involved in disputes.

The work of the security services is far from glamorous.
The image of jet-setting James Bonds is pure fantasy,
though as we shall see later, much of the James Bond tech-
nology is real enough. Most of the work of the security
services involves low-level information-gathering and is mind-
grindingly dull. It concerns cutting articles out of newspapers
and magazines and filing them away for future reference,
probably never to be used.

MI5 and MI6 (the 'MI' is an acronym for Military Intelligence) are officially known as D15 and D16 (Defence Intelligence) but for the sake of consistency I will refer to them
by their better-known titles.

MI5 is theoretically responsible to the Home Office and
MI6 to the Foreign Office. Both agencies work closely with
Britain's biggest Intelligence-gathering organisation, the
Government Communications Headquarters at Cheltenham.
GCHQ monitors and intercepts radio broadcasts worldwide,
military and civilian, official and unofficial, and employs
thousands of people 24 hours a day on tape-recording, trans-
lating and code-breaking.

It is through GCHQ that Mrs Thatcher learned of the
Argentine orders to the *Belgrano* to change course and
return home. The organisation is officially part of the
Foreign Office but is in reality under the control of the
United States worldwide eavesdropping organisation, the

National Security Agency (NSA). The NSA actually has two major electronic surveillance centres of its own in Britain: the larger is at Menwith Hill in Yorkshire and the other is at Morwenstow, near Bude in Cornwall. Both centres monitor international telephone calls, business and private. *All* international phone calls—even your Christmas Day greetings to overseas relatives—are tape-recorded and studied to see if they pose a threat to the security of the United States government.

The headquarters of MI6 are at Century House, 100 Westminster Bridge Road, London SE1. MI5's headquarters are at Curzon House, Curzon Street, W1.[1] The Special Branch is based at New Scotland Yard.

If you want to write to MI5 to report your next-door neighbour as a subversive you can do so at its 'front office' address: Box 500, 14-17 Great Marlborough Street, W1.[2] The current Director General of MI5 is Sir John Jones, soon to be replaced by Sir Anthony Duff.[3] Because the information you have just read is an official secret you should now turn yourself in!

Both MI5 and MI6 have many properties throughout Britain and overseas, but most of their London offices are in Mayfair, hardly a cheap area. As they are funded through the so-called 'secret vote' of senior civil servants, and as Parliament is never told how much they cost to run, we can only guess how much taxpayers' money goes towards their upkeep. A recent estimate (March 1985) put it at £1 billion per year.[4]

On 25 September 1952 the Tory Home Secretary, Sir David Maxwell-Fyfe, issued a directive to the Director General of the security services which, for the first time, outlined the way in which MI5 was supposed to be accountable to Parliament. It said:

1. In your appointment as Director General of the security services you will be responsible to the Home Secretary personally. The security service is not, however, a part of the Home Office. On appropriate occasions you will have right of direct access to the Prime Minister.
2. The security service is part of the defence forces of the country. Its task is the Defence of the Realm as a whole, from external and internal dangers arising from attempts

at espionage and sabotage, or from actions of persons and organisations whether directed from within or without the country, which may be judged to be subversive of the State.

3. You will take special care to see that the work of the security services is strictly limited to what is necessary for the purposes of their task.

4. It is essential that the security services should be kept absolutely free from any political bias or influence and nothing should be done that might lend colour to any suggestion that it is concerned with the interests of any particular section of the community, or with any other matter than the Defence of the Realm as a whole.

5. No inquiry is to be carried out on behalf of any Government Department unless you are satisfied that an important public interest bearing on the Defence of the Realm, as defined in para. 2, is at stake.

6. You and your staff will maintain the well-established convention whereby Ministers do not concern themselves with the detailed information which may be obtained by the security service in particular cases, but are furnished with such information only as may be necessary for the determination of any issue on which guidance is sought.[5]

Even if we generously accept that MI5 has since interpreted this directive as meaning it should defend only the *status quo* against radical change, it is now abundantly clear that the security services are not 'absolutely free from any political bias'. The label 'enemy within', which Prime Minister Margaret Thatcher applied to the 180,000 miners who went on strike in 1984, now applies to most of us. According to the National Council for Civil Liberties (NCCL), the Police National Computer holds more than 36 million entries—'the equivalent of one for nearly each adult member of the community'.[6]

The loudest whistle to be blown on MI5's current activities was that of Cathy Massiter. Ms Massiter was a former MI5 agent who resigned from 'F Branch' (responsible for spying on industrial subversives) in protest at the blanket surveillance of groups like the Campaign for Nuclear Disarmament and the NCCL, including one NCCL official, Harriet Harman, who subsequently became a Labour MP.

Things were fairly bad 30 years ago, when MI5 spied on
15 Labour MPs. The surveillance included tapping their
telephones, opening their mail and gaining copies of their
bank statements. Information about the MPs was actually
requested by three leading members of the Labour Party at
the time: Hugh Gaitskell, George Brown and Patrick Gordon
Walker.[7] Later, the then Labour Prime Minister, Harold
Wilson, told the *Daily Telegraph* on 12 April 1967: 'When
we came into office naturally I found out what was going on.
I felt that the system of the previous government, in which
MPs' telephones were being tapped, should be changed.'

Whether Mr (now Lord) Wilson, did in fact change the
system remains in doubt. The General Secretary of the
National Union of Seamen, Jim Slater, claims to have
evidence which shows his members were made the subjects
of intensive Intelligence-gathering activities during the bitter
seamen's strike of 1966. Harold Wilson, of course, was Prime
Minister at the time.

The Wilson government is also believed to have sought
information about trade union leaders after the General
Election of February 1974 in order to sew up the Social
Contract which helped limit pay rises.

Jack Jones of the Transport and General Workers Union,
and Hugh Scanlon of the Amalgamated Union of Engineering Workers, were spied on by MI5 in 1972 and information passed directly to the then Prime Minister, Edward
Heath, instead of through the 'official' channel of the Home
Office.[8]

According to one MI5 agent, who worked in the 5th
floor tape-recording room at Curzon House, pressure groups
and active trade unionists were under routine surveillance
throughout the 1970s. She claims that the miners' leader,
Arthur Scargill, used to shout abuse down the telephone at
the MI5 agents who were monitoring his conversations. She
says the Scottish miners' leader, Mick McGahey, also had
his telephone tapped and that an engineering union leader,
Ken Gill, actually had his house broken into so that a more
sophisticated bug could be planted to monitor every word
that was said in his home.[9]

Many radicals in Britain have at some time suspected they
were under surveillance. On 3 February 1980, *The Observer*
reported that three Labour MPs were convinced their tele-

phones were tapped. They were former Junior Ministers,
Michael Meacher and Bob Cryer, and the man who is now
leader of the Parliamentary Labour Party, possibly the next
Prime Minister—Neil Kinnock. We can only speculate as to
how Mr Kinnock might seek to reform the security services
if he succeeds in his ambition.

Tapping the telephone is extremely easy. One of the most
authoritative documents on the subject was published in
July 1980 by the Post Office Engineering Union:

> Most members of the public would be amazed and con-
> cerned by the range and sophistication of surveillance
> technology which now exists. Most official tapping—
> whether authorised by warrant or not—is carried out on
> behalf of the relevant agency by specially selected Post
> Office personnel. These personnel volunteer for the task
> and are drawn from grades represented by a number of
> trade unions (including, of course, the POEU). During
> their time on tapping duties, they are under the operation-
> al control of the Home Office.

Although the POEU has retained its historic title, most telephones in Britain are now operated by British Telecom, or
BT, which in 1984 was taken away from public ownership
and sold into private hands. Nevertheless, the POEU report
on the telephone tappers is still relevant.

'These men,' it said, 'are unknown to their other Post
Office colleagues and operate out of their sight and in most
cases without their support. The ordinary Post Office
engineer has nothing whatsoever to do with telephone tapping and has the same mixed feelings about this practice as
most members of the community.'

The POEU report said a telephone conversation could
be intercepted at any point between two subscribers. It continued:

> In practice, most parts of the transmission line plant
> would not be used for tapping purposes, since in
> many cases tapping circuits would present formidable
> technical and practical problems. Interfering with a
> cabinet, pillar or distribution point in the local network
> would be too open to public view and too liable to dis-

covery by Post Office engineers on normal duties.
Therefore, most tapping takes place in the local telephone exchange or in the customer's premises.

In the case of official tapping, virtually all of it is liable
to be based on the exchange since, compared to a home
or office, access is easy and detection is unlikely. It is unlikely that such official tapping is based on the main
distribution frame where each individual circuit is wired
across by a jumper lead.

The main points to note about this procedure are that
it is possible to gain easy access to the exchange outside
normal hours and work in reasonable comfort with
little chance of being observed. The basic operation is
simple and quick. It is easy to pass the tap to the monitoring centre (which may be any distance away) via a
trunk or junction circuit by the use of one jumper. No
attention is drawn to an extra jumper since there are
already so many, and there is little prospect of discovery
by staff on conventional duties.

The main monitoring centre for MI5, MI6 and the police is
at 113 Grove Park, Camberwell, London SE5. The only
entrance is via an electronically-operated steel doorway.
Officially, the centre is part of the C7 Division of the Metropolitan Police, which supplies technical services, but
according to the local planning register it is a 'wireless rec-
eiving station'. The R12 division of British Telecom, based
at Martlesham Heath near Ipswich, specialises in research
and development and works closely with GCHQ.[10] It is
responsible for producing some of the more sophisticated
surveillance techniques listed in the POEU report:

1. A conventional tap on a telephone line which may be
a metallic contact or an induction device which picks up
the pulse in the line—these draw an almost undetectable
amount of electricity from the telephone wire and give
no betraying noises.
2. An 'infinity transmitter' which is a device inserted into a telephone handset which, when activated by
dialling the number and giving an ultrasonic note on the
last digit, prevents the telephone ringing and transmits
over the dialler's line all the sounds in the room where

the telephone is situated, whether the handset is on or off the telephone—this can be installed in a matter of minutes.

3. An induction device to pick up telephone conversations from the stray magnetic field of the telephone itself—this must be within about four feet of the telephone.

4. A microphone using a wired link, the wired link either being specially laid or using an existing pair of wires or a single insulated wire—the range and sensitivity is unlimited depending on the size of the microphone.

5. A microphone using a radio link with a transmitter—the sensitivity is great although the transmission range is limited.

6. An electronic stethoscope of high amplification with wall-listening microphone and socket for connecting pin-hole microphones or the spike-mike for inserting into plaster walls—this requires access to adjoining walls.

7. A directional microphone concentrating a beam of sound from a distance on to a sensitive microphone and so hearing across intervening noises—the range is only about 25 yards.

8. Reflection of a laser-beam off a window-pane or an object in a room to pick up the vibrations generated by the speaker.

The POEU went on: 'Many of these techniques are used by the police and the security services. No warrants are needed to employ bugs in a police investigation—in the Metropolitan Police, bugging is normally authorised by a Deputy Commissioner . . . most of these techniques are practised by those organisations and individuals concerned with industrial espionage or private investigations.'

According to *Observer* journalist Nick Davies, an expert on the security services, MI5 routinely breaks into people's homes to plant bugging devices or seek information. He says MI5 has a whole section of 'professional cracksmen' whose sole concern is breaking and entering.

'The locksmiths and carpenters are from a section known as A1(D) and the burglars from A1A,' he says. 'Their calm assumption that they may ignore the criminal law is one of the central elements in the row which now threatens to engulf MI5.'[11]

Telephone tapping and mail interception are supposed to be authorised by a ministerial warrant when they concern a perceived threat of subversion. However, as has become painfully clear during the row over Cathy Massiter's allegations, the definition of subversion now covers almost everyone who is not a card-carrying member of the Conservative Party. It is also clear that warrants, when issued, cover not just individuals but organisations.

Fortunately, the spooks are human (some of them — the bulk are computers) and make mistakes. In July 1972 they were caught out for spying on the anarchist weekly newspaper, *Freedom*. This form and official envelope were wrongly delivered to the newspaper instead of to the Special Branch. Forms like this are used by local post offices when handing over packets of mail for opening to regional offices. For the record, it is not a crime to be an anarchist or to publish a newspaper.

P 811X (Spl)

ADVICE OF DESPATCH & FORM OF RECEIPT
(for special items on non-financial nature only)

CPD (S.S.) Post Office,
Room 202, Union House,
St. Martin's le Grand,
London, EC1A 1DQ.

17 JLY 1972 19

The o/c
EDO (PD) The undermentioned special items are herewith.
~~Have been sent to you today.~~

(6)

Please acknowledge receipt below and return this form completed to me at the above address.

RECEIPT

The CPD (S.S.),
Receipt acknowledged.

OFFICE STAMP
19

NOTE.—This form should be used where acknowledgement is specially desired of the receipt of items or documents of a special or confidential nature, etc., but not for the acknowledgement of the receipt of money or the equivalent of money.

815/934 970947 20M 5/72 FHB Ltd. 815

(reduced)

```
No. 40

                              EXPRESS
IMMEDIATE


            THE  OFFICER  ON  DUTY,
                INVESTIGATION  DIVISION,
                    (SPECIAL  SECTION),  POST  OFFICE,
                        ROOM  202,  UNION  HOUSE,
                             ST.  MARTINS-LE-GRAND,
                                   LONDON,  E.C.1.
POST OFFICE
```

(reduced)

A former chairman of the Conservative Party, the MP Cecil
Parkinson, once indiscreetly admitted to the journalist Chris
Mullin that he had a security services' file on the political
views of several leading members of the Campaign for
Nuclear Disarmament. Mr Mullin says[12] this confirmed his
long-held suspicion that MI5 was supplying senior Tories
with information about anti-nuclear protestors for party
political reasons.

Another journalist, Anne McHardy of *The Guardian*,
claims she was told by an aide to the former Northern Ireland
Secretary, Roy Mason, that her telephone was tapped. She
says the aide knew all the details about a row she had with
her husband on the telephone and when she asked how he
came by the information he told her: 'I've been listening to
the tapes. We've been following you, too.'[13]

It seems there are few of us who are not potential targets
for telephone tapping. Unfortunately, although it is easy to
tap a telephone, it is very difficult to prove that a telephone
is tapped. It is possible to buy anti-bugging devices which
pick up electro-magnetic pulses from any hidden
microphones but many are unreliable. As the POEU report
put it: 'Private bugging and efforts at de-bugging are now
big business. Equipment is easily available and last year
(1979) an American company, Communication Control
Systems, actually opened a London shop selling a wide

variety of specialised devices. The shop is called "Counter-spy" and is located at Park Street in Mayfair.'

MI5 and the Special Branch also devote much of their time to infiltrating radical organisations. Cathy Massiter claims to have controlled one such 'mole' — a man who had been active in Left-wing circles for 30 years called Harry Newton. He was actually treasurer of the Institute for Workers' Control when he was sent to infiltrate CND. Mr Newton died in 1983 and his friends and relatives were deeply shocked by Ms Massiter's allegation that he was in fact a spy. Another 'mole', Ronnie White, claims to have infiltrated the National Front and taken part in beating up blacks in order to make Intelligence reports to the Special Branch.[14]

The most recent Home Office guidelines on how the security services should operate says only that they should not target groups or individuals simply because they espouse 'unpopular causes'. Unpopular with whom?

As far as the Government, the Special Branch and MI5 are concerned, Hilda Murrell was someone who espoused unpopular causes — peace and conservation to name but two. Was her telephone tapped because she supported CND? Or because she supported Greenpeace and Friends of the Earth? Or may be because of her active involvement with the Llanymynech Rocks Nature Reserve?

Until more people like Cathy Massiter come forward, we will never know if, or why, Hilda Murrell was under surveillance. All we know is that it is *possible* she was under surveillance. But that in itself should be cause for grave concern.

A Tiger by the Tail?

QUIS COSTODIET CUSTODES?

The reason why so many people believe Hilda Murrell might have been killed by a person or persons connected with the security services is because they know that such an act is possible. Some would doubtless go further and claim that it is actually probable. Confidence in MI5 and the Special Branch is at an all-time low.

The examples of MI5 abuses quoted in the previous chapter are but a tiny sample of the available evidence; the security services, MI5 and the Special Branch in particular, are completely out of political control.

The Government is currently legislating to regulate telephone tapping. It is doing so because it has been forced to by the European Court of Human Rights, which in August 1984 ruled that the British police had acted illegally when they tapped the telephone of antiques dealer James Malone. The Government hopes that the Interception of Communications Bill will prevent any similar embarrassment. There seem to be few safeguards built into the legislation; indeed, there is some evidence to suggest the Government is actually taking the opportunity to make matters worse.

One clause in the Bill says that a person's telephone may be tapped if they are engaged in activities which pose a threat to the 'economic well-being' of the State. What on earth is that supposed to mean? Is it not a thoroughly subjective term, open to interpretation as MI5 sees fit?

In my view, the biggest threat to our economic well-being is posed by American-based multi-national corporations, the Confederation of British Industry and Mrs Thatcher—but do they have their telephones tapped?

The only sensible way to operate a secret service within a democracy in peace time is specifically to prohibit *all* telephone tapping, infiltration of trade unions and pressure groups and so-called 'counter subversive' measures unless there is clear evidence that a crime has been or is about to be committed.

Groups like CND, NCCL and Greenpeace are quite lawful. So are trade unions. Even the Communist Party, Sinn Fein and the National Front are constitutionally acceptable in a democracy, although the latter should perhaps face more prosecutions than it does in view of its declared racialist propaganda and policies.

Hilda Murrell was certainly no criminal, not even in the twisted imagination of MI5 agents. Yet it is likely that she was under surveillance.

In March 1985 the chairman of the Security Commission, Lord Bridge, said he could find no evidence of any unauthorised activity by MI5. This announcement caused few surprises because Lord Bridge had been specifically told by the Government not to look for any. His terms of reference had been to study *only* that activity which had been authorised by ministers.

No one has suggested that any minister at any time asked the security services to burgle Hilda Murrell's home. Tam Dalyell believes the decision was taken at a 'fairly low level' and that MI5 chiefs will have learned about it only when the burglary attempt went so tragically and fatally wrong.

If this is correct, it means that MI5 is not only unaccountable to ministers, but that it has lost control of itself. Yet Prime Minister Margaret Thatcher, in a letter to Opposition Leader Neil Kinnock,[1] made it clear she still has the utmost faith in the way MI5 operates. 'It is for the Home Secretary and me to satisfy ourselves that the security services operate entirely within the letter and spirit of its directive,' she said, referring to Sir David Maxwell-Fyfe's 1952 instructions to MI5. Mrs Thatcher said she attached 'the greatest importance' to the directive. 'We accept this responsibility,' she continued, 'which I assure you is fully discharged, as it always has been. I do not believe there are any grounds for changing the present system of accountability to ministers which has stood through successive governments.' And yet the present system of accountability is one of complete non-accountability. If the system has stood unchanged throughout successive governments, then the time has now come for Lord Wilson and James Callaghan to tell us exactly what was going on when they were Prime Ministers. That is, of course, if they know.

The whole question is very much in the melting-pot, with pressure growing for some sort of supervisory committee to relieve ministers of the burden of keeping the security services in check. The problem is wittily expressed in what the former United States President Lyndon Johnson once said of his FBI Chief Edgar Hoover: 'I would rather have him inside the tent, pissing out, than outside the tent, pissing in.' Ministers have been reluctant to reform MI5 for fear that, like Frankenstein, it would turn on its supposed master.

The idea of broadening responsibility for the security services is not new. In 1983 Tam Dalyell told the House of Commons: 'The time has now come for the establishment of at least a British equivalent of the United States Senate Intelligence Committee. The proposal is neither way-out nor far-fetched.'[2] MPs from all sides of the House of Commons are currently coming to terms with the need for a select committee to monitor MI5, possibly composed of Privy Councillors from all parties.

Without some mechanism whereby the security services are to be held accountable, MI5 and the Special Branch will continue to be accused of illegal telephone tapping and spying activities, and will continue to lose the confidence of the citizens they are supposed to defend. We can only guess as to whether such matters ever weighed on the mind of Hilda Murrell. What is certain is that her murder has forced us to think about them.

Afterword

Since work on this book began there have been some interesting, possibly unrelated sideshow developments.

Following a telephone conversation between myself and the publishers on 19 February, the publishers' north London house was broken into. Nothing was stolen, although a gold watch and £60 cash had been clearly available. Late at night on Friday, 1 March, after I had arranged by telephone to spend the weekend in London, my neighbours in Cornwall saw a prowler in my garden. They set their dog on him and he ran away over a field. The incident was puzzling because the village where I live has a very low crime rate.

On 20 March, I was visited at my home by the Assistant Chief Constable of Northumbria, Peter Smith, and his colleague, Supt Cecil Hall. As part of their review of the

West Mercia police handling of the murder inquiry they wanted to talk to anyone who might have information about the case. Although it is very flattering for a humble journalist to have his views sought by two senior policemen, I was unable to provide them with any new evidence relating specifically to the murder. Nevertheless, neither Mr Smith nor Mr Hall raised any objection when I explained my criticisms of the West Mercia police. They said many people had made similar complaints but would not be drawn on their own opinions. They added that part of their review of the case would include interviewing 'anyone – literally anyone, who might have some kind of information.' When I asked if this would include the private detectives who had been spying on the Sizewell objectors, Mr Smith replied: 'We said anyone and we meant anyone.'

I told them that they should take very seriously anything they might be told by Tam Dalyell, MP, and said that if I had the resources I would myself look far more closely at how Barrie Peachman seems to have shot himself. That, dear reader, is what I now urge you to do.

22 March 1985

References

Chapter 1

1. *Shropshire Star*, 26 March 1984; interviews with Rob Green, February/March 1985.
2. 'World in Action', Granada TV, 4 March 1985.
3. Det. Chief Supt David Cole, evidence at inquest, 5 December 1984.
4. Interview with author, March 1985.

Chapter 2

1. Inquest transcript.
2. Inquest transcript.
3. *Shropshire Star*, 26 March 1984.
4. Inquest transcript.
5. *Shropshire Star*, 26 March 1984.
6. *Shropshire Star*, 26 March 1984.
7. Inquest transcript.
8. BBC TV 'Crimewatch', 14 March 1985.

9. Inquest transcript.
10. *Shropshire Star*, 23 May 1984.
11. *Shropshire Star*. 2 April 1984.
12. *Shropshire Star*, April 1984.
13. *Shropshire Star*, May 1984.
14. *Shropshire Star*, 3 July 1984.
15. *Shropshire Star*, 12 September 1984.
16. Inquest transcript.

Chapter 3

1. A Home Office pathologist who, for obvious reasons, wishes to remain anonymous.
2. Inquest transcript.
3. Interview with author, March 1985.

Chapter 4

1. Notably Harlech TV, 'World in 'World in Action', *New Statesman* and *Observer*.

2. Notably London *Standard*, 15 March 1985 and Press Association.
3. *Shropshire Star*, 29 March 1984.
4. Home Office minister Giles Shaw, *Hansard*, 17 December 1984.
5. 'World in Action', Granada TV, 4 March 1985.
6. *Observer*, 6 January 1985.
7. *Observer*, 6 January 1985.
8. *Shropshire Star*, 19 April 1984.
9. BBC TV 'Crimewatch', 14 March 1985.
10. Letter to the author, March 1985.
11. 11-page police statement issued to press, January 1985.
12. 'World in Action', Granada TV, 4 March 1985.
13. London *Standard*, 7 February 1985.
14. London *Standard*, 7 February 1985.
15. 'World in Action', Granada TV, 4 March 1985.
16. *New Statesman*, 11 January 1985.
17. *Observer*, 6 January 1985.

Chapter 5

1. Interview with author, March 1985.
2. Interview with author, March 1985.
3. Transcript of Sizewell B public inquiry, 1983-85.
4. *New Statesman*, 25 January 1985.
5. 'World in Action', Granada TV, 4 March 1985.
6. 'World in Action', Granada TV, 4 March 1985.
7. BBC TV 'Crimewatch', 14 March 1985.
8. *New Statesman*, 8 March 1985.
9. *Daily Mirror*, *Labour Weekly*, February 1985; *Searchlight*, March 1985.
10. Channel 4, '20/20 Vision', March 1985.

Chapter 6

1. Interview with author, March 1985.
2. *Hansard*, 19 December 1984.
3. *Hansard*, 19 December 1984.
4. *Hansard*, 19 December 1984.
5. 'World in Action', Granada TV, 4 March 1985.
6. *Hansard*, 19 December 1984.
7. Letter to Tam Dalyell, 28 December 1984.

8. *Observer*, 6 January 1985.
9. *Observer*, 6 January 1985.
10. 'World in Action', Granada TV, 4 March 1985.
11. Letter to author, 12 March 1985.

Chapter 7

1. *Hansard*, 19 December 1984.
2. *Hansard*, 19 December 1984.
3. *Hansard*, 19 December 1984.
4. *Hansard*, 19 December 1984.
5. *Hansard*, 19 December 1984.
6. *Hansard*, 19 December 1984.
7. Quoted by the Press Association, 15 March 1985.

Chapter 8

1. 11 January 1985.
2. West Mercia Constabulary press officer, Alan Peach.
3. BBC Radio 4, 'PM', 4 March 1985.

Chapter 10

1. Interview with author, 9 March 1985.
2. Letter to author, 10 March 1985.

Chapter 11

1. Series of articles by Duncan Campbell in the *New Statesman*, February 1979-January 1981.
2. Duncan Campbell.
3. *Observer*, 17 March 1985.
4. *New Statesman*, 8 March 1985.
5. Quoted in *The History and Practice of the Political Police in Britain*, by Tony Bunyan, 1977.
6. *Privacy: the Information Gatherers*, by Patricia Hewitt, 1980.
7. *Inside Story* by Chapman Pincher.
8. *Observer*, 10 March 1985.
9. Channel 4 TV, '20/20 Vision', March 1985.
10. Duncan Campbell.
11. *Observer*, 10 March 1985.
12. Letter to *The Guardian*, February 1985.
13. Channel 4 TV, '20/20 Vision', March 1985.
14. Channel 4 TV, '20/20 Vision', March 1985.

Chapter 12

1. Letter to Neil Kinnock, 1 March 1985.
2. *Hansard*, 17 November 1983.